# Robert Froman

Robert Winslow Froman was born in 1917 on a ranch near Big Timber, Montana, and grew up in Caldwell, Idaho. He attributes his education chiefly to the Carnegie Public Library in Caldwell and to Reed College in Portland, Oregon. In 1945, after jobs on *Time, Tide* and other magazines, he became a free lance. He has contributed some two hundred articles to *Collier's, This Week,* the *Saturday Evening Post,* and other magazines.

*One Million Islands for Sale* is Mr. Froman's first book. He and his wife, Elizabeth Hull, also a writer, live on a farm within easy reach of Manhattan; they have so many and such hospitable island-owning friends that they haven't yet gotten around to buying an island of their own.

# One Million Islands for Sale

ROBERT FROMAN

# One Million Islands for Sale

*A guide to more than one million islands for sale or for rent around the shores and in the lakes of the United States and Canada*

Duell, Sloan and Pearce · *New York*
Little, Brown and Company · *Boston*

DUELL, SLOAN AND PEARCE—LITTLE, BROWN
BOOKS ARE PUBLISHED BY
LITTLE, BROWN AND COMPANY
IN ASSOCIATION WITH
DUELL, SLOAN & PEARCE, INC.

*Published simultaneously*
*in Canada by McClelland and Stewart Limited*

PRINTED IN THE UNITED STATES OF AMERICA

*To*
*ELIZABETH*

# Preface

I DISCOVERED, conquered and settled briefly on my first island at the intrepid age of eleven. It was about thirty feet long, half that wide, and surrounded by the two-foot-deep, summer-stagnant waters of the Boise River near my home town of Caldwell, Idaho. After dislodging the aboriginal muskrats, I had a fine Robinson Crusoe time until my parents found me out and decided that even two feet of water was enough to drown in.

In spite of that early experience I later fell victim to the widespread delusion that private islands are attainable only by the very rich. It was the 1948 announcement by the War Assets Administration that it had for sale several abandoned island forts off the Atlantic coast which started me dreaming of islands again. I dug up a big atlas and tried to locate the W.A.A. islands.

To my surprise and delight I found that the New England coast alone seemed to have dozens of islands. Later, on large-scale sailing charts, I discovered that the dozens actually were thousands. Other large-scale maps of the rest of the continent showed hundreds of thousands more.

That discovery launched me on the most difficult job I ever have undertaken. Over the last ten years I have covered hundreds of stories for various national magazines, and many of those stories have been on complicated scientific and industrial subjects. But reporting on them was simple compared to the task of gathering the facts on the islands of North America.

They are so numerous, so widely scattered and so endlessly varied that it would take several lifetimes to explore them all. What I have had to settle for is a sort of sampling. I have spent four years on the task and have sought to make the book as complete and authoritative as possible. Even so, the size of the task probably has made errors of commission and omission inevitable. I would like to appeal to any readers who note such errors to tell me about them.

Each chapter after the introductory first one gives a general description, with specific examples, of the islands of one region. At the end of each chapter I have listed sources of additional information, including some of the real-estate dealers who handle island properties. (These lists are solely for the convenience of readers, are not represented as complete and are not intended as endorsements, recommendations or guaranties of any kind.)

Since buying an island usually means buying a boat with which to reach it, I have included in the appendices a list of boat builders and price lists of various types of boats. These lists are by no means exhaustive, but they will give you an idea of what is available and of what it costs. (Again, they are not intended as endorsements, recommendations or guaranties of any kind.)

The appendices also include advice on a number of other points more or less peculiar to islands. I have relegated this advice to the back of the book because it won't interest all readers. But for anyone concerned with any of the matters covered I think the information will come in handy.

I have not included any maps because, paradoxically, they would have made the book quite impractical. Many of the most interesting small islands appear on even large-scale maps only as nondescript dots. Such a dot may be a useless, barren rock, or it may be the answer to someone's prayers for a peaceful, quiet haven. To make the dots meaningful I would have had to include so many maps of such large scale that the book would have become a small library. You can find in any good atlas the area in which the islands which most interest you are located. Local government agencies in most areas can furnish you more detailed maps of their localities if you want them.

One other glaring type of omission is that of the exact locations and of the names of the owners of some specific islands discussed. These omissions were made at the request — in some cases, at the vehement demand — of the owners of these islands. Any publicity, they insisted, would destroy their privacy, and complete privacy is for them the chief purpose of owning an island.

But most of the hundreds of islanders with whom I talked and corresponded were so enthusiastic about their way of life that they were delighted to tell all. I owe each of them my thanks, which I hereby sincerely extend. A number of them have given me so much time and encouragement that I would like to make specific acknowledgment:

To Mrs. June Burn of Waldron Island, Washington; Mrs. John Cederquist of New York City; John Stuart Cloud of Boston and Inner Green Island, Maine; David B. Conover of Wallace Island, British Columbia; Captain Percy A. Cook of Scotch Plains, New Jersey, and Cook Island, Florida; Mr. and Mrs. Charles Davis of New York City and Pine Island, Maine; Walter F. Downey of Boston and Birch Island, Maine; the Honorable John Foster Dulles of Washington, D. C., and Main Duck Island, Ontario; Ed Fitzgerald of Hay Island,

Connecticut; S. F. Hill of Columbus and Seminole Island, Ohio; Miss K. C. Kittery of Garnerville, New York; Stephen A. Lavender of Thomaston, Maine; Gurdon Leete of New York City; Mrs. Richie C. Magee of Altamont, New York, and Outer Spectacle Island, Maine; R. K. Malcolm of Liberty Island, California; Edward J. Noble of New York City, the Thousand Islands and St. Catherine's Island, South Carolina; Mrs. Gertrude Gray Single of West Hartford and Governors Island, Connecticut.

In addition, I would like to thank the numerous officials and employees of government agencies who have taken the time to answer the endless questions I put to them. I would like to acknowledge, in particular, the help of T. J. Courtney of the Nova Scotia Bureau of Information; William Dougherty of the United States Department of the Interior; Miss Josephine Hemphill of the United States Department of Agriculture, and J. E. Wright of the Ontario Department of Travel and Publicity.

I also want to make acknowledgment to the editors of the *Saturday Evening Post* and of *The Story of Our Time,* published by The Grolier Society, Inc., in which articles of mine based on some of the material in this book have previously appeared.

R. F.

*Garnerville, N. Y.*

# Contents

# Contents

# One Million Islands for Sale

CHAPTER I

# Islands for Sale

In the fall of 1948 the New York office of that great grab bag, the War Assets Administration, announced plans for one of the most unusual of all the thousands of sales of surplus government property. The office was ready to accept bids, it said, on half a dozen islands scattered along the Atlantic coast between Maine and New York. The islands were obsolete for coastal defense purposes, and the government was anxious to be rid of them.

Overnight the office's startled staff members found themselves transformed from government clerks into glamorous guardians of the keys to a set of earthly paradises. On the morning after the announcement appeared in the newspapers the waiting room was jammed by more than a hundred would-be Robinson Crusoes. All day long the telephone jangled incessantly. For weeks afterwards floods of letters poured in.

"All I want," wrote one wistful hopeful, "is just a little island where I can get away from it all for the rest of my days."

"I want an island quick," another scribbled on a postcard. "Will be in next week with the money."

Altogether there were some twenty-five hundred excited

inquiries. Nearly all of them seemed to be based on a wide-spread delusion. "All my life," as one woman put it, "I've dreamed of owning an island. This is probably the only chance I'll ever have to buy one, so please don't sell before I get there."

A corollary to this is the idea that islands are primarily rich men's toys. "Next to having your name included on a list of wealthy tax dodgers," one society reporter has written, "one of the most easily recognized hallmarks of opulence is ownership of an island."

Even society reporters are seldom more absurdly mistaken in their assumptions. At the moment there are more than one million quite habitable islands for sale or rent in and around the United States and Canada. You can buy some of them for as little as ten dollars an acre. You can lease others up to a thousand acres in area for twenty-five dollars a year. They lie scattered along the coasts and in lakes and rivers all the way from the Gulf of Mexico to Alaska. Some are tame and easily accessible. Others are as wild and remote as anyone with a mind to escape from civilization could want.

Actually, one million plus is merely an estimate of the absolute minimum of habitable North American islands. There may be twice that many or more. No one has ever attempted to count them individually. Even the various state and provincial governments which retain ownership of most of them have only the vaguest ideas of the numbers within their domains.

Few are complete with ravishing and ravishable native girls, meals to be had for the plucking from breadfruit or mango trees, and the general paradisaical atmosphere usually associated with the fabled South Sea isles of romance. But then neither are the South Sea islands so equipped except in the fables.

Neither the imaginary paradise nor the less appetizing

reality bears any resemblance to what you will find among North American islands, but even so the variety is enormous. One type is the sea island of the coast of New England and the Maritime Provinces. There are between four and five thousand of these. Most are now privately owned, but a few are always for sale at prices as low as three or four hundred dollars. Usually covered with spruce or fir, they often have rocky shores which make them difficult to approach. In winter they mostly are strictly for Viking types, but in summer the climate is ideal.

Near the opposite extreme are the low, sandy, semitropical islands of the Florida and Gulf coasts. Estimates of the number of these range as high as half a million, but the great majority of them are either too swampy or too dry to be habitable. Thousands, of course, hover on the border line and can be hauled back across it if you have the pioneering spirit. A few such can be leased from state governments. But most of the more desirable ones are privately owned, and prices depend on the types of houses which have been built on them.

In most of the eastern part of the continent, lake and river islands are far more numerous than coastal ones. The Canadian province of Ontario, in fact, may have all by itself more than a million habitable islands, probably the world's greatest concentration of small bodies of land surrounded by water. Most are Crown property, and the provincial government is glad to sell them to either Canadians or United States citizens. The price is a flat forty-five dollars per acre with a limit of ten acres to a family and a requirement that a certain amount of building be done on the property during the first year or two after purchase.

Perhaps the most famous of our inland archipelagoes is the Thousand Islands, located at the point where Lake Ontario empties into the St. Lawrence River. Actually, the chain includes more than seventeen hundred islands, two thirds in Canada and the rest in New York State. Their beauties have been touted for more than a century, but they are difficult to exaggerate. A sort of crystal clarity seems to pervade the whole area. On windless days the St. Lawrence is so clear that you can see the sandy bottom even in the deepest parts.

All this once was available only to the extremely wealthy, but the last depression changed all that. Many of the islands now fall well within reach of middle-income pocketbooks. Of a few dozen recently listed for sale by a real-estate dealer in the area, one which is small and houseless could be had for five hundred dollars, and others with houses and utilities were in the range from five to ten thousand dollars.

In the center of the area is one of the most fabulous of all private islands — Heart Island and its Boldt Castle. More than half a century ago George Boldt, famed nineteenth-century hotelkeeper and owner of New York's old Waldorf-Astoria, bought the island and had it reshaped in the form of a heart as a wedding anniversary present to his wife. He also imported cornices, towers, staircases and other parts from dozens of European palaces and had them assembled into an enormous gingerbread of a castle. Just before the project was completed, and after Boldt had spent more than two million dollars, his wife died. He sent a telegram to the contractor calling a halt to the finishing touches then being put on the castle and, according to legend, never once visited the place. Today it is merely a sight to be seen by tourists.

South and west from the Thousand Islands area, along the United States side of the Great Lakes, islands are much less plentiful than on the Canadian side. But even a state as solid-looking as Ohio seems on the maps has at least a few hundred lake and river isles. Many are only a fraction of an acre in area and barely a hop and a skip from shore. But they are nonetheless genuine islands, and life on them is entirely different from life on the mainland. Just ask one of their owners — and stand by for a few full-blown dithyrambs.

"You don't realize what an island can mean until you've lived on one for a while," a Columbus, Ohio, businessman explains earnestly. His is located on a tiny lake seventy miles from Columbus, and he spends every week end, holiday and vacation he can take on it the year round.

"The minute I step ashore on the island — well, it's hard to explain. I get a sort of feeling of calm and contentment. It's like magic, as if being surrounded by water cuts off all my usual worries. Then I get out my rod and reel, and life is beautiful."

The most heavily islanded area in the Midwest is northern Minnesota. A single twenty-mile-square section contains over a hundred lakes which in turn harbor more than a thousand islands. Of late prices in this area have been going up with three- or four-acre unimproved islands selling for as much as twenty-five hundred dollars. More remote ones are a good deal cheaper, however. If you know how to use an ax and can sustain a rugged mood long enough, most of these have plenty of fine timber for building your own cabin.

In the South and Southwest there are no great concentrations of islands, but a surprisingly large number of individual ones can be found tucked away in odd corners. A few in the Mississippi River are subject to squatters' rights while they last, which usually is only between one spring flood and the next. They often are worth the trouble of an annual move, though, for almost anything will grow luxuriantly on the alluvial mud of which they are made.

Even the Rocky Mountain area has a few islands to offer. Some of them are almost islands in the sky, being found in lakes a mile or more above sea level. But because of the sharp drop of its ocean floor, the United States Pacific coast has far fewer islands than the Atlantic side of the continent. California has only eleven habitable sea islands, and Oregon claims not a single one.

One of the most attractive island groups in the whole country, however, is in Washington's Puget Sound. Altogether, the Sound has more than 350 islands, but the pick of the lot are the 172 San Juan Islands strewn along the northern reaches just south of the Canadian border. They range from a family-size acre or so up to several square miles in area, but they are all more or less alike in their as yet unexploited serenity.

Unfortunately, World War II brought the Puget Sound area such an influx of population that property values have soared. One beach homesite on a San Juan island was sold for only five hundred dollars in 1938. In 1949 it changed hands again for ten thousand.

Just across the international border to the north, however, along the coast of British Columbia, begins an archipelago of thousands of magnificent islands, many of which are still vacant and under ownership of the provincial government. Like Ontario, British Columbia will sell to either Canadians or Americans, but the price here starts at a rock-bottom ten dollars per acre. Mostly scattered through the four hundred miles of the Strait of Georgia and Queen Charlotte Sound, which separate the large bulk of Vancouver Island from the British Columbia mainland, the islands recently have been discovered by Americans in large numbers, and the more southerly ones are going fast. But the climate of the whole area is equable the year round, and there are hundreds left further north.

Southern Alaska has another couple of thousand islands similar to those of British Columbia, though somewhat more remote. Most of them are under the jurisdiction of the United States Forest Service, which won't sell but will lease at a top price of twenty-five dollars a year.

Some say that with a little ingenuity and a great deal of determination a man could live off the soil and surrounding sea of a southern Alaskan island. The mean winter temperature is about the same as that of Washington, D.C. Venison from the particularly toothsome Sitkan deer and a wide variety of game birds would guarantee a meat supply. There are half a dozen kinds of trout in the fresh-water streams, and you would go a long way to find better salt-water types than the spectacularly fighting coho salmon, the halibut and the black sea bass.

And of course, Alaskan islands are not without a few hazards to add spice to a life on them. Perhaps the spiciest item is the Alaskan brown bear, which has invaded the islands there in force. Weighing up to twelve hundred pounds, nasty-tempered and much too fast for comfort, these formidable brutes have almost doubled their numbers in the last two decades. Although they ordinarily eat berries, grubs and fish like good little bears, they also go in for an occasional meal of good red meat. There is no indication that they have developed an ungovernable lust for *filet d'homme*, but there are a number of well-authenticated cases of their having carved up human intruders on their domains.

All of which is undoubtedly far too strenuous for many dreamers of dreams about islands. In fact, almost any effort apparently would be too great for some prospective Crusoes who seem to have formed intimate connections in their minds between the idea of life on an island and the idea of utter laziness.

One of the W.A.A.'s callers the day after the announcement of the island sale was of this persuasion. A distinguished, elderly gentleman wearing a white Vandyke beard and a Homburg, and carrying a cane, he swept majestically into the office and buttonholed one of the clerks.

"I understand that you are offering Great Gull Island for sale," he said, referring to one of the abandoned defense posts near New York. "I may be interested. May I ask what kinds of trees grow there?"

After going over the list of the island's features, the clerk assured him that there were no trees of any kind.

"No trees!" the old gentleman snorted. "No trees at all? Why, that's absurd. In that case I can assure you that I am not interested. The only reason I want an island at all is to sit under the trees in peace and quiet."

With which he turned and stalked out indignantly.

Other reasons for wanting islands frequently are just as special as this subarboreal one. One of the W.A.A.'s correspondents wrote that he was constantly being tempted to embark upon a life of crime and that the only thing that could save him would be retirement to an isolated island. Another said that she had been racking her brains to think of an appropriate birthday present for her husband and had decided that an island was just the thing. Still another wrote that he would buy one only if it came equipped with cellars guaranteed atom-bomb-proof.

Most, however, simply echoed the well-known Garbo expression of the desire to be without company. Although the letters came from all over the country and all types of people and were written on everything from embossed linen to brown wrapping paper, the chief group represented seemed to be professional men. Nearly all were in quest of a vacation home where they could live for part of the year in moated isolation from the demands of their clients. Oddly, the profession most heavily represented was that of dentistry, proof perhaps that it does hurt the man behind the hand that holds the drill as much as it hurts the one behind the tooth that gets drilled.

The enthusiastic response to the W.A.A. announcement clearly proved, in any case, that islands are the ideal escape ports in the minds of those who have had enough of time tables, shoving crowds and the other appurtenances of civilization. Unlike many popular conceptions, this one is quite accurate.

Consider a New York City couple, for instance, both schoolteachers, who own an island in Maine. Their island, which they never have bothered even to name, consists of only a little more than an acre of wooded land in a lake near Augusta. But every summer, when they slough off the accumulated frustration and fatigue of a year of teaching and retire to the island, they lead for three months a life which is about as close to that of the Garden of Eden as modern man can approximate.

It is only half a mile from shore at the nearest point, and three miles up the lake from the village which is their source of supplies. A leaky boat with an ancient outboard motor is the only means of transportation they need. And once ashore on the island they are completely sovereign and independent, at least for the time being, of the rest of the world. Host, hostess and guests relax without giving a thought to what the people next door may think for the excellent reason that there is no next door.

Sometimes, of course, this independence can result in a certain eccentricity, for an island's isolation provides plenty of room for the development of its owners' peculiarities. One group of Boston Brahmin families has owned an island off the Massachusetts coast for many years. To an outsider an invitation there signalizes the granting of a passport to Boston society. After one visit, however, most male guests have been quite happy to surrender their passports. Presumably for the purpose of proving that the Puritan spirit still lives, it is the unalterable rule that every man present must take a dip in the ocean at six o'clock every morning regardless of the weather. Only an authentic case of double pneumonia, attested by an acceptable physician, is considered an excuse, and a rather feeble one at that.

But for most people the effect of island life seems to be more on the soothing and relaxing side. That certainly has been the result in the case of Betty MacDonald who, in *The Egg and I*, made her literary reputation out of her boundless detestation of the chicken and all its works. Some time ago she and her second husband were reported buying a farm on Vashon Island near Seattle. More recently it has been further reported that they have started raising chickens on said island.

One of the most outlandish of all stories of the softening effect of island life comes from Guernsey, one of Britain's Channel Islands. It concerns a Guernsey rent collector who, after thirty-six years on the job, finally prepared to retire. When he set forth on his last round of tenant dunning, he was perplexed to find no one at home until he reached the last house on his route. There he found all his collectees gathered, waiting to present him with a huge memorial clock. It bore an inscription proclaiming him the ideal rent collector.

Nothing quite so far gone in peace and good will ever has been reported from North American islands. In fact, almost nothing at all has been reported from — or about — any of them except for a few notorious ones such as Manhattan and its adjacent Long and Staten Islands, Alcatraz, Key West and suchlike. One of the chief reasons for the lack of reportage is that the great majority of our islands are hidden away in nooks and crannies of the continent. Many of them are so well hidden that the United States Coast and Geodetic

Survey admits quite frankly that it doesn't know how many islands there are even in the limited areas along the coasts which fall within its domain.

It is this concealment and lack of publicity, of course, which explain the large number of islands still available for sale or rent. But the same factors make finding the island you want a problem in exploration. This book, so far as I know, is the first attempt even to estimate the total number of North American islands, not to mention providing any sort of guide to them. With more than a million islands to cover, it won't be possible to describe more than a small fraction of the total in detail. But each chapter will include all the essential particulars of the islands of one large area, beginning with those of Canada's Maritime Provinces and proceeding first down the Atlantic Coast to the Gulf, then across the continent to the Pacific, winding up with the remote and fabulous islands of British Columbia and southern Alaska.

Each chapter also will include the stories of island owners and dwellers in the area, men and women who have made come true the dream of escape to a fair, far island. Again excluding inhabitants of such altogether unprivate islands as Manhattan, there are probably between fifty thousand and one hundred thousand fortunate souls who have found island homes, some only for part of the year but others for the year round. They range from teen-agers to retired couples in their eighties, from summer vacationers through dirt farmers, fur breeders, resort operators and sellers-of-sea-shells-by-the-seashore to full-time hermits, from down-and-out squatters to millionaires.

If the island fever ever grips you and carries you out of your armchair on an island-hunting expedition, the stories of those who have made successes of their homes on the diverse types of islands of the various areas will help you decide at least which part of the continent you want to start on. In each area there are a number of short cuts to be pointed out for island seekers. In most areas there are ways of giving island life a trial before committing yourself, and a variety of experts who can be consulted about just which hidden cove or stretch of open sea you should investigate.

Unfortunately, there is one way in which it no longer is likely that you will be able to acquire an island — namely, by simply discovering and claiming it. One of the last men to succeed at this was a young American sailor named Jennings, whose story marks the height of success in beachcombing.

In 1856 Jennings's ship, an Antarctic-bound whaler, stopped in Samoa to take on supplies before the final plunge into the frozen polar seas. Just before it sailed, Jennings quarreled with the captain and jumped ship. For some reason he made a hit with the Samoans and soon married a daughter of one of the chiefs. But it was necessary for him to disappear before his ship returned, lest he be picked up for desertion.

He and his wife and a few Samoan friends set off across the open sea in canoes. Several days later they landed on a fertile, uninhabited atoll and acquired ownership simply by moving in. They made it the independent Kingdom of Jennings, without coinage, taxes, jails or any of the other trappings of civilization. It remained that way until 1935 when, on the application of the fourth- and fifth-generation descendants of Jennings and his friends, it was formally annexed by the United States of America.

Jennings's was among the last few habitable islands in the world not under the sovereignty of one or another of the great nations. It isn't possible to obtain quite as high a degree of independence as his on an island here at home, but you can come reasonably close.

Buying an island, however, is like buying anything else.

You can be stung badly if you don't know the angles. One of the most important items to be on guard about is, oddly, the water supply. Though an island is a body of land surrounded by water, it often happens that the only way you can obtain a drop to drink is by catching the rain. This is more often true on sea islands than on river or lake ones, the surrounding water itself frequently, though not always, being drinkable on the latter.

A good example of the horrible worst that can happen was the Army's experience on Great Gull Island, off the eastern tip of New York's Long Island. Drilling for wells was attempted in twenty-six different places. One was carried to a depth of 1826 feet. The drills came up bone-dry. In the end the island's water supply had to be carted to it daily in tankers — a project which would bankrupt most private island dwellers.

Another important item to consider is transportation of yourself and supplies to and from the island. Only in a few heavily settled island areas such as the Thousand Islands is there dependable water taxi service. Elsewhere you must count the cost of a boat as part of the island's purchase price. And if you have to cross any long stretch of open sea, it will have to be a good-sized, sturdy and expensive boat.

Also, you will need docking facilities for the boat, and this means that your island should have some sort of cove or inlet sheltered from rough weather where you can build a dock. Without some such natural harbor you may have to build a breakwater, again a probably costly proposition. Your trouble will seem quite unnecessary in good weather. But once a blow comes up you will find, unless you enjoy the prospect of being marooned indefinitely, that your every thought will be for the boat and how it is riding out the storm.

Then there is the problem of choosing between a large

island with room for several houses and a small, single-family one. The disputes between partisans of big and little islands sometimes generate large numbers of thermal units. Big-island enthusiasts say that the little-islanders are affected purists and that it is idiotic to reject the conveniences made possible by several families' sharing expenses. Champions of little islands say that the big-islanders are gadget-crazy and might as well go on back to the mainland whence they came. They insist that only an absolutely private island makes any sense. It is, obviously, a controversy which everyone must settle to please himself, but it's a good idea to listen to the arguments at length before making up your mind.

In some areas — particularly along the Atlantic and Gulf coasts — it's also a good idea to take a long look at an island before you put any cash on the line. During the last century several dozen islands have completely disappeared from these coasts, and others have been whittled down to mere stumps by swift-flowing currents. When Sharps Island in Chesapeake Bay was first surveyed a hundred years ago, for instance, it covered 445 acres. Since then two whole villages gradually have been washed away. Now the island measures less than a hundred acres.

There is, however, another side to this business. In some areas of low, flat, sandy islands, the currents instead of washing away the land sometimes add to it by piling silt and sand against the exposed edges. Off Louisiana some of the low-lying islands seem to travel about, their substance eroding away at one end and simultaneously building up at the other.

But such difficulties as no drinking water, no harbors, and erosion, you can discover fairly easily and quickly. Others which are confined to individual islands — a noisy foghorn on a nearby lighthouse, for instance, or plagues of oil washing up on the beach from passing ships — take a long time to find out about. Consequently, it's a good idea to rent before buying if you possibly can.

Before you decide to set out on the quest, though, be warned that once the island fever grips you it may not let go. Consider the example of a Los Angeles family. A few years ago these people drove to Seattle and spent a week with friends living on one of the Puget Sound islands. When they returned home, even the supposedly irresistible charm of Southern California couldn't erase the memory of the peace and quiet of their island days.

The following summer they arranged to rent one of the Puget Sound islands for a month. And the year after that they sold their California home, bought the island and settled permanently on it.

If you are perfectly satisfied where you are and don't want to feel otherwise, it might be a good idea to close the book now and forget about it. But on the other hand, you may find between these covers a map of the road which will lead to the life you have always dreamed of living.

CHAPTER II

# Islands of the Maritime Provinces

Straining out to sea from the northeastern tip of the United States, Canada's Maritime Provinces — New Brunswick, Nova Scotia, Prince Edward Island and New-foundland — are freely exposed to the battering of the North Atlantic in its frequent wild and windy moods. Storms, ice-bergs and rip tides have battered and slashed at these coasts for centuries. In the process they have carved out thousands of islands, ranging in size from rocks which barely clear the water to Newfoundland, which is half the size of Great Brit-ain. Some are close inshore and well protected, while others lie many miles out and are freely exposed to the worst the ocean can do.

All four provincial governments are glad to be helpful to Americans, since tourist dollars provide substantial parts of their incomes. Usually, you will find that you can own or lease property on terms at least as favorable as are available to Canadians. If you propose to set up on your island a resort or other attraction which will draw Americans, local authorities often will go to considerable lengths to help you.

Exploring the islands of the Maritimes will take you far off the beaten track. You can drive to New Brunswick and Nova Scotia on new and fairly good roads, and there's a car ferry to Prince Edward Island. But from the main centers, to which the highways lead, you'll usually find that the only way to get to the islands is via a back road to a fishing village where you can hire a boat.

## Newfoundland

Still farther out of the way, of course, is Newfoundland, which you can reach only by boat or plane. (You can ferry in a car, but most of the roads are primitive and they cover only a small part of the province.) If it's privacy you want, though, you can certainly find it on one of the little islands which ring the province. There are so many that the Crown Lands Division of the Department of Natural Resources in St. John's, which controls them, will estimate only that they "number thousands." Few of them even have names.

Few of them offer anything in the way of creature comforts, either. In fact, although the initial cost of buying or leasing would be low, the cost of building anything more than a rough cabin which you could put together with your own hands would be multiplied by the remoteness of many of the islands. It would take a minor expedition to get in materials and workmen, and expert organizing to keep the place stocked with food and other supplies.

But if you really want to get as far away from it all as possible and if you have either plenty of cash to spend (meaning, probably, several thousand dollars) or a passion for rough living, a Newfoundland island summer home may be your dream come true. In most cases, however, only a super-pioneering spirit would prevent the dream turning to nightmare in winter, if you tried to make a year-round home of it. For the Arctic Ocean is only a hop and a skip up the globe. July's mean temperature is 60°, and 90° is almost unheard of. But the best the province's publicists can say about the winters is that the thermometer "seldom registers below zero."

From May to September, though, you can catch all the hard-fighting Atlantic salmon and sea trout you can carry. In many of the bays small whales and porpoises will come right up to your doorstep, and harpooning them is supposed to be great sport. Stately icebergs may also float by, providing magnificent though slightly chilling spectacles. And in September you can round out the season with a moose hunt.

Provincial authorities are so enthusiastic about attracting Americans that they will give you all the help they can. This is quite rare, for islands usually are so remote and difficult to track down that the authorities know little and care less about them.

"I feel sure," writes a Department of Natural Resources official, "that interested persons could select a desirable location were they to visit the country. In contacting this Department for information on islands I would suggest that parties state whether they require islands situated inland or coastal and indicate what recreational facilities they consider essential to the area."

The Province of Newfoundland includes the coast of Labrador, a much-broken twelve-hundred-mile stretch with literally uncounted islands. So far as I have been able to learn, however, none of them is for sale, the reason being that no prospective buyers of island real estate on this hard, frozen coast ever have turned up. About the only reason for buying one would be as a long long-term investment. If the meteorologists who say the earth's climate gradually is growing warmer are correct, a Labrador island might conceivably be of value to your great-grandchildren's great-grandchildren.

## St. Pierre and Miquelon

Just off the southern coast of Newfoundland lie the tiny, rocky islands, St. Pierre and Miquelon, which are all that's left of France's once great North American empire. There are a few still tinier and rockier islands belonging to them, but none is advertised as for sale or even as habitable. The chief attractions of this bit of old France are the splendid fishing for salmon and sea trout and the opportunities for buying French and other European goods tax-free. Perfumes which sell for fifty dollars in New York can be had at St. Pierre for eight. Sixty-five-dollar Swiss watches cost only fourteen, and five-dollar wines go for as little as forty cents.

Rumrunning once was the chief occupation of many local "fishermen." The natives like to tell tales about their adventures with the United States Coast Guard in those good old days. Now the authorities are trying to regain some of the lost income by attracting United States tourists, and a visit to the place will give you a taste of life on a remote island.

## Prince Edward Island

Like Newfoundland, Prince Edward Island makes up a province of Canada all by itself. But its more sheltered location in the Gulf of St. Lawrence gives it a considerably milder climate. It covers about twenty-two hundred square miles and has a population of around a hundred thousand, many of whom are descendants of the so-called United Empire Loyalists who left their homes in New England and New York in 1784 in order to remain under the British flag. Like many remote outposts of empire, it is more British than Britain.

There are only a few small islands scattered around Prince Edward's coasts. One in Hillsboro Bay on the southern shore was offered for sale by its private owner, but it's on the bleak side. The same goes for most of the others. The best use for them would be as sites for hunting lodges. They offer very nearly the world's best duck and goose shooting.

It was on an island in Cascumpeque Bay on the northern shore that a man named Charles Dalton many years ago worked out one of the favorite ways of making a living out of a small private island. Dalton got hold of a few pairs of foxes, turned them loose on the island and made a fortune. In fact, his idea was so good and his foxes flourished so fruitfully that, instead of selling the furs, he sold breeding pairs to other islanders. Some of his customers did the same, and the business of growing foxes on islands eventually spread all the way to Alaska. It's no business for an amateur, however, and probably as many fortunes have been lost in it as have been made.

Another product of this area is the famed Malpeque oyster, named for the bay in which it is grown. For a couple of hundred years it has been a favorite with gourmets. Prince Edwardians modestly call it "the world's most perfect oyster," and there are many who agree with them. The harvest is small, and only a few are exported.

## Nova Scotia

Among the Maritime Provinces, Nova Scotia is your best bet for an inexpensive and comparatively easy-to-reach island. Some 370 miles long and sixty to a hundred miles wide, the province is entirely surrounded by water except for the narrow isthmus, Chignecto, which connects it with New Brunswick. Cape Breton Island, about a hundred miles long, forms the northeastern tip of Nova Scotia and is separated from it by the half-mile-wide Strait of Canso. It's so remote and unspoiled that many of the Scots who make up the bulk of its population still speak Gaelic.

The province's climate is similar to New England's, though it claims slightly cooler summers and warmer winters. It lies exactly halfway between the equator and the North Pole, and its publicists call it "the sea-conditioned province." Its forty-six hundred miles of jigsaw coastline varies from great, gray, granite cliffs to tree-capped, sloping headlands to long stretches of red and white sand beaches with villages, devoted mostly to fishing, scattered along at frequent intervals. According to provincial authorities there are at least fifteen hundred definitely habitable islands plus several hundred others, the habitability of which is less certain.

Some are Crown lands, which means that they are owned by the provincial government. At present the province is maintaining a "no-sale" policy, but it will lease island properties, chiefly for camping purposes. Such leases are available mostly among islands in inland lakes and streams. The area leased usually is restricted to one acre although the law permits up to five acres. The charge is fifty dollars for a ten-year lease, and lessees are given an option for renewal.

Many of the most desirable coastal islands are in Mahone and Tusket Bays on the side of the province which faces the open Atlantic. Nearly all of these are privately owned. One of the most intriguing is Outer Baldonia, three treeless acres well out in Tusket Bay. Every September it becomes for a week or so a fisherman's Utopia. Its full name is the Principality of Outer Baldonia, and its owner, Russell M. Arundel of Warrenton, Virginia, styles himself the Principality's Prince of Princes.

Arundel bought the island in 1949 and dedicated it to an annual "Tuna Tournament" for himself and a few friends. An important feature of the tournament is a prize for the most intelligent-looking fish caught. But more important are the long sessions of conviviality in the Principality's three-room palace.

"None of us," Host Arundel boasts, "ever has taken a fish of any appreciable size."

According to local real-estate dealers, most of the other owners of islands in this group are local citizens who would be receptive to offers from outsiders because they dream of making the area a vacation center. One Yarmouth agent says of the Tusket Bay area at the southern tip of the province: "Anyone who wants an island can come and pick his own as to size, place and condition." And the purchase price of some might be only a few hundred dollars if you handled the deal right. But the cost of making all but the exceptional bargain habitable probably would be many times that amount.

One of the Tusket group was being offered for sale some time ago at an asking price of fifteen thousand dollars. It lies three miles off the mainland and covers several acres. It has a dock, three small cottages and the shell of a large lodge, unfinished inside. You probably would have to invest in a large and seaworthy cabin cruiser to get to and from the island, though you might be able to arrange for transportation with a commercial fisherman at one of the mainland villages.

Tusket Islanders in particular and Nova Scotians in general claim that they can offer the world's best blue-fin tuna and broadbill swordfish angling plus excellent duck hunting. They say that eight-hundred-pound tuna are commonplace.

They also say that it was in Tusket Bay that the sport of

tuna fishing got its start, and they make a fine fish story of the claim. It was in 1871, the story goes, that a local school-master wound several hundred feet of ordinary cod line on a swivel reel, fashioned a large hook of steel, and set out in a dory in search of a blue-fin. A large specimen co-operatively took the hook. But as soon as it felt the line, it started circling the bay at top speed and finally flung the dory into the midst of a fleet of herring netters, swamping one of the latter and thoroughly tangling the nets. The tuna got away when an apoplectic herring fisher cut the line. But the schoolmaster told his story in a British magazine for fishermen, and the sport was launched.

Another big attraction of the Nova Scotia islands (if you are attracted, that is, by the idea of doing a little digging) is of a sort usually associated with the tropical islands of the Caribbean. It seems to be fairly well established that the privateers of colonial days frequently used Nova Scotia islands as bases. It is somewhat less firmly established, but not less firmly believed by many modern islanders, that buried pirate treasure still remains to be uncovered on many of the islands.

Most celebrated of these island treasures is that of Oak Island in Mahone Bay. The treasure is "said" (by whom and with what authority no one seems to know) to have been buried by Captain Kidd. But no matter who did the interring, something in the way of a treasure definitely was concealed underground on the island back in the days of the pirates.

It was in 1795 that three mainlanders went duck hunting on the island and saw an old ship's block hanging from the limb of a big oak tree in a position which seemed to indicate that it had been used for derricking something extremely heavy. In the soil beneath the block was a depression about ten feet in diameter. The hunters forgot all about ducks and rowed back home to get shovels.

According to the story they hit a layer of oak planks at a depth of ten feet. At twenty feet there was a second layer, and at thirty there was a third. These tantalizing planks continued to turn up and urge the diggers on every ten feet all the way down to a depth of ninety feet. For a final teaser, the last layer was covered with putty. Then, at ninety-six feet, water rushed in and flooded the pit.

During the next one hundred years Oak Island was a treasure hunter's Mecca, but every attempt to go deeper was defeated by the underground water channel. In 1900 some optimist set up a drilling rig and succeeded in pushing borings down to 150 feet. He found three broken oak chests and a few coins of eighteenth-century mintage. That, of course, set off a new wave of digging. So many shafts have been sunk since that no one is sure just where the original hole was dug. A theory has been advanced, however, that in the course of a century and a half the gradual shifting of underground sand may have moved the treasure a long way in almost any direction. If you want to have a try, you have as much chance as anyone.

Altogether, there are supposed to be 365 islands in Mahone Bay. (For some reason this figure of 365, or a leap-yearish 366, is the favorite of almost everyone who counts or estimates the number of islands in any given area.) In any case, Mahone Bay does have upward of three hundred islands, mostly habitable and many for sale. Prices range from a few hundred to several thousand dollars, depending chiefly on the number and state of the buildings. The bay is protected from the open sea to some extent, and you could get by with an open outboard motorboat for transportation to and from some of the islands close to shore.

To the south of Tusket and about eighteen miles out at sea lies an island which is as remote and isolated a bit of water-girt real estate as the most determined escapee from civilization could ask. Lying low on the sea and covered with scrub spruce, Seal Island is about three miles long and half a mile wide. It's near the mouth of the Bay of Fundy, and until sixty years ago it was a death trap for ships caught in fogs, storms, or the rip-roaring Fundy tides.

At that time two mainland families moved out to the island, lived by fishing and saved the lives of dozens of castaways. In fact, they helped so many castaways live to tell the tale of the danger the island presented to navigation that the Canadian government finally was moved to build a lighthouse and end the wrecks.

Today the island — except for two hundred Dominion-owned acres at its southern tip where the lighthouse stands — is the property of a widow descended from one of the original two families. At last report she was prepared to sell it, although not anxious to do so, and it had to be to the "right person." One stipulation was that the commercial fishermen from the mainland who occasionally stop to rest at one end of the island during the December-to-May season must continue to have this privilege.

The best way to prospect for a Nova Scotia island would be to drive to the province by car and follow the coast highway #3 along the Atlantic side from Yarmouth north to Halifax, a distance of 212 miles. This will take you past the two chief island concentrations in Tusket and Mahone Bays and several smaller groups. There are still more remote and less developed island concentrations along the coast northeast of Halifax if you want to continue in that direction along highway #7. Both #3 and #7 follow the coastline closely and overlook the Atlantic at many points.

## New Brunswick

This province, which borders Maine on the east, claims far fewer islands than Nova Scotia. It has a considerable number of lake and river islands. "But," says one provincial authority, "they are decidedly not for people who want to get away from it all. The islands are usually either very sandy or of a rich soil suitable for raising hay crops. In both cases they usually are low-lying and are submerged and badly mauled almost every year by spring freshets."

There are, however, a few of even these inland islands and several groups of coastal islands which would make fine hideaways. Among the most interesting are Campobello, Deer and the Grand Manan group, the latter consisting of one large and a dozen smaller islands. All are located at the mouth of Passamaquoddy Bay, which separates New Brunswick from Maine. A few of the smaller Grand Manan group, ranging from ten to a hundred acres in area, are just about the right size for a single family and might be for sale at fairly stiff prices. But the chief appeal of this group is to those who want their isolation diluted by the presence of a few other escapees.

Best known is Campobello, which was for several decades the summer home of President Roosevelt's family. A group of old American families, including the Roosevelts from New York, bought large parts of the island in 1881, built summer homes there and made it an extremely exclusive social center. It still has some of the stateliness inherited from those days, but there are now even a few tourist homes on the island. The Roosevelt estate, a fifteen-acre hilltop with a large mansion, was sold in July, 1952, to Armand Hammer of New York, head of the Hammer Galleries, who told a reporter that he was buying it "as an investment." That presumably means that it will be for sale again sometime, but the price — not to mention the upkeep — probably will be rather forbidding to nonmillionaires.

Deer Island, farther up Passamaquoddy Bay, is somewhat less grand but equally quiet and reposeful. It consists of alternating fir forests and vivid green meadows, neat little villages with comfortable big homes and wide lawns and everywhere the sea pulsing in and out through deep estuaries. There are a good many tourist accommodations and homes or homesites at fairly reasonable prices.

Grand Manan is the most remote of these three large islands, lying about eight miles out in the Bay of Fundy, but there's a regular ferry service (as there also is to Campobello and Deer Islands). The island is about twenty miles long by ten wide. On the side facing the mainland it presents a continuous line of towering cliffs rising sheer out of the water to heights of as much as four hundred feet. But it slopes down from these heights toward the seaward shore. Most of the island life, including six small villages, and all the smaller islands, are located on the southeastern side.

Seals, porpoises and occasional whales are among the chief sights to be seen off the island. It's also a big ornithological center, specializing in an enormous variety of seagoing birds such as puffins and stormy petrels, and it has several stations for scientific biological and oceanographic study. It attracts a good many summer visitors, but it's still well off the beaten track and far from crowded.

Another island area is Northumberland Strait, which is farther north between New Brunswick's eastward coast and Prince Edward Island. For various complicated climatological reasons the water of the Strait is warmer than that of the rest of the region, where it's often too cold to swim even in August. But the Strait is not too warm to harbor lobster and the famous Atlantic salmon, a fish which many sportsmen rave about.

Unfortunately, many of the best salmon-fishing areas have been leased by, or otherwise reserved to, private clubs of fishermen. What makes this particularly regrettable, from the point of view of nonmembers, is that this is one of the world's hardest-fighting game fish as well as one of the most toothsome once you get it into a pan. It's also one of the most difficult to persuade to take a hook.

A friend of mine who has fished for salmon on the Upsalquitch River, at the northern tip of New Brunswick where it adjoins Quebec, has a tale to tell about this last point. He spent a whole morning a few years ago at a big clear pool on the river where the water was so clean and quiet that he could see a dozen big salmon floating around in obvious boredom. But every fly he could think of, including a number he invented on the spot, seemed only to leave them more bored.

Finally he fell into a rage, picked up a rock and heaved it at the fish. Instantly, three of the biggest salmon flashed up from the bottom of the pool and began fighting over the rock as it sank.

"It made me so damn mad," my friend says, "that I almost jumped in and tried to strangle them with my bare hands."

There are the usual unknown number (at least several hundred) of islands scattered along the Strait, most of them close inshore and not requiring too large an investment in a boat for transportation. Many of them are for sale either as a whole or in part. Here's a real estate agent's description of one:

Shediac Island in Shediac Bay used to harbor about forty farm families. They have all drifted away, most of them to work in the towns during World War II. The island is about a mile long and half a mile wide, has rich soil and good stands of timber. Summer, beginning in June and lasting through mid-September, is pleasant and winter mild with little snow, but I can say nothing in favor of our extremely damp spring.

I have for sale a portion of the island ninety acres in extent, part of which is cleared, part wooded with a mixture of soft and hard woods. The acreage extends down to the shore on both sides, and the beach is excellent. The only undesirable feature I have seen about the property is that mosquitoes are, in certain seasons and under certain weather conditions, prevalent. I am satisfied, however, that a small amount of proper swamp draining in other parts of the island would wipe out the mosquito.

There are buildings which housed a lighthouse keeper in years gone by. These buildings, however, probably will have to be torn down as they are not suitable for anyone who would be likely to buy the property and live there during the summer months. A purchaser would also have to provide water and electric light and any other facilities of such a nature. The northern end of the island is one third mile from the mainland, the town of Shediac being five miles away from the landing point. The island's southern end is one quarter mile from the mainland, and it's another mile and a half from the landing point to Point du Chêne, a summer colony. The island's owner will sell for $5500.

Further north there are available islands in Miramichi Bay and off Bathurst, which is on the Baie de Chaleur. This is another big hunting and fishing area with a plenitude of ducks, geese and, on the mainland, deer and moose. One agent who handles properties in the Baie writes a perhaps ominous note about a deal he recently made there: "I recently sold a fifteen-hundred-acre private island here. However, it may be for sale again soon."

Of the province's lake islands, the few of much interest are those near the Maine border. One large lake with a number of islands, about fifty miles north of Campobello and not far from a Canadian Pacific Railway stop, is Magaguadavic (if you ever ask for it, you'll be glad to know that the local pronunciation is Magadavy). The lake and its shores are full of trout, moose, deer and other game. And at least one island in the lake, Wildwood, probably would be for sale to a substantial bidder. It has a comfortable lodge and docking facilities.

One of the oddest islands anywhere on the shores of the continent is located about eleven miles southwest of Grand Manan Island and ten miles off the Maine coast. Named Machias Seal Island, it's a quarter-of-a-mile-square rock, utterly bleak and barren. Probably no one would have any interest in it except for the fact that it's one of the few specks of land anywhere on the globe that is not definitely a part of one nation or another. No one seems sure whether it is part of the United States or Canada.

A couple of years ago the New York *Times* asked its correspondents to query various government authorities in both countries about ownership of the island. The result was a wonderful tangle of high-level contradictions.

A Dominion of Canada official in Ottawa: "Machias Seal Island is in Maine."

Provincial officials in St. John, New Brunswick: "It's Canadian territory, officially a part of New Brunswick."

The official State of Maine position: "Machias Seal Island is American."

The Canadian Information Office in New York City: "Apparently it's in the United States."

The Navy's hydrographic charts: "Foreign territory."

United States Coast and Geodetic Survey charts: "United States territory."

The United States State Department (which, perhaps justifiably, seemed to feel that this was *one* hullabaloo it didn't want to get involved in): "There is, in this matter, an unresolved problem."

All of which would seem to make the island a fine place for someone with a spirit of adventure — and a battery of good lawyers — to establish as an independent kingdom by judicious assertion of squatters' rights. Unfortunately, it's too late. The Canadian government long ago decided that, no matter who owned the island, it was the ideal place to build a lighthouse to warn against the surrounding shoals. The three tenders of the light, however, might conceivably get away with declaring their independence. Probably no one would notice.

## Sources of Additional Information

NEWFOUNDLAND

> Newfoundland Tourist Development Office
> Fort Townshend Square
> St. John's, Newfoundland, Canada

ST.–PIERRE AND MIQUELON

> M. le Gouverneur du Territoire
> St.-Pierre
> Territoire des Iles St.-Pierre et Miquelon
> (You'll probably receive an answer in French.)

PRINCE EDWARD ISLAND

> P.E.I. Travel Bureau
> Charlottetown
> Prince Edward Island, Canada

NOVA SCOTIA
  *General*
    Bureau of Information
    Provincial Building
    Halifax, Nova Scotia, Canada

  *Real-Estate Agents* (their addresses indicate the areas in which
      they specialize):
    Mrs. Phyllis Walker
    Caroline Real Estate Company
    Chester, Nova Scotia, Canada

    Harbour Realties
    53 Commercial Street
    Dartmouth, Nova Scotia, Canada

    John J. Brittain
    Pyne Block
    Digby, Nova Scotia, Canada

    D. J. Fraser
    Grant Block
    Yarmouth, Nova Scotia, Canada

NEW BRUNSWICK
  *General*
    New Brunswick Travel Bureau
    Fredericton
    New Brunswick, Canada

  *Real-Estate Agents*
    Earl T. Caughey
    St. Andrews
    New Brunswick, Canada

    Guy R. Day & Son
    St. Stephen
    New Brunswick, Canada

C H A P T E R   I I I

# Islands of Ontario and Quebec

THESE TWO VAST PROVINCES, together more than three times the size of Texas, have within their borders the continent's greatest concentration of islands. In fact, they have more islands than any other region of comparable size on earth. Only a few are coastal islands. The rest are scattered among the millions — literally millions — of lakes which dot the two provinces.

Both provinces, of course, stretch far to the north, and large parts of both — in fact, most of Quebec — are Arctic or sub-Arctic in climate. Thousands of miles of their northern boundaries lie on Hudson Bay. But hundreds of thousands of square miles of their southern areas have excellent summer climate and winters at least no worse than New England's. And in those areas, within easy reach of Eastern and Midwestern United States by plane, train or car, you can have your choice among islands of all shapes, sizes and conditions for as little as forty-five dollars each.

## Quebec

Although Quebec is the larger of the two provinces, a much greater portion of its area is too far north to be of much interest to anyone not inclined to the Eskimo way of life. There are, however, numerous lake islands in the temperate southern part of the province which would make excellent summer retreats. The provincial government takes little interest in these islands. It had not, at last report, clamped a "not for sale" policy on those it owns, but it doesn't offer much encouragement, either.

"We do not advertise our islands as being for sale," says one provincial official, "as is done in other sections of the Dominion. However, if anyone wishes to purchase an island in the Province, and it is available for sale, he is welcome to do so. There is no legal impediment to the purchase of any Quebec island by an American citizen."

I have been unable to find anyone who negotiated the purchase of an island from the provincial government. But there are a number — perhaps several hundred — of now mostly privately owned islands in the Quebec section of the St. Lawrence River, and many of them have been developed as summer vacation havens. Near Sorel, about forty miles down the St. Lawrence from Montreal, there's a group of more than one hundred small and medium-size islands. Cottages on several of them with the whole island, or with only a part in the case of some of the larger ones, "might be" for sale, meaning, if you offer enough. Several of those furthest from the river banks have not yet been built on and would come fairly cheap.

There's a similar river island concentration thirty miles down-stream from Quebec City near the town of Montmagny. At the last report I received, one large island there was definitely for sale, but it wouldn't come cheap. Named L'Ile aux Oies — Goose Island — it's 1650 acres in extent, with nine hundred under cultivation and the rest in woodland. There are nine farmhouses and ten barns plus several other buildings, good springs and wells, a gravel road running the length of the island and several windmills for generating electricity and pumping water. It's a natural game preserve where thousands of migratory waterfowl stop every year and has impressive views of the Laurentian hills to the north. It's no cozy retreat, and the agent handling it is aiming at a purchaser who would turn it into either an exclusive and expensive club or a vacation camp for the employees of some large corporation.

Farther down the St. Lawrence River, where it begins to widen out into the Gulf of St. Lawrence, are a few more isolated islands but no large groups. Most are large, and so far as I have been able to learn none is for sale as a whole. I have been able to learn even less about the Magdalen Islands group far out in the Gulf. They are extremely remote, lying about halfway between Prince Edward Island and Newfoundland. But their names — such as Coffin Island and Grindstone Island — don't sound very promising. There are a number of fishing villages with more intriguing names, though — Havre Aubert, Etang du Nord and Pointe Basse — which prove at least that the islands are not completely uninhabitable.

## Ontario

In the Province of Ontario you will find one of your best chances of buying a private but easily accessible island cheap. If you want an island for a summer vacation home and if you live in the northeastern quarter of the United States, you should, perhaps, investigate the Ontario islands first of all. Many of the province's chief island concentrations are less than six hundred miles — a long day's drive or a couple of hours' plane flight — from even such southerly points as St. Louis and Richmond, Virginia. Thousands of Midwesterners and mid-Southerners, not to mention Pennsylvanians, New Yorkers and New Englanders, already have established summer homes — in some cases year-round homes — on their own islands in Ontario's lakes. But there is room for many tens of thousands — in fact, hundreds of thousands — more such private island homes.

The province stretches from a southern latitude parallel to that of Eureka, California, to a northern boundary in the same latitude as Ketchikan, Alaska. Its easternmost point is almost as far east as New York City and its westernmost is west of Minneapolis. In that vast spread of territory, provincial authorities estimate, there are at least two million lakes. Most of them have at least one island, and others have thousands. In Georgian Bay, the northern arm of Lake Huron, there are thirty thousand islands.

Naturally, many of the islands in the more northerly lakes are of little interest unless you are determined to leave civilization far, far behind. You would have to be extremely determined, too. There's occasionally snow in July along the province's Hudson Bay coast.

But after eliminating most of the northern two thirds of the province, there still remain countless islands. Because even this drastic narrowing down still leaves so many and such varied islands to deal with, this chapter will not be concerned with either the Thousand Islands, which Ontario shares with New York State, nor the islands in the lakes of the far western part of the province. Both will be dealt with in later chapters — the Thousand Islands in Chapter VI and those of western Ontario in Chapter IX.

Jumping-off points within easy reach of all the islands to

be dealt with in this chapter are readily accessible by good highways or by railroad. At many such jump-offs you'll find water taxi service available to take you to your island. But even if you have to provide your own water transportation, an inexpensive outboard motorboat is all you will need. You can also get by with a canoe or rowboat if you are budget-cramped and feel venturesome.

If you want to do further investigating before you make an island-hunting trip to Ontario, provincial authorities will be glad to answer any questions you have and to supply you with maps and descriptive literature. They are anxious to encourage Americans to travel and vacation in the province, and they will go to considerable trouble to help you. And the province is by far the world's biggest dealer in island real estate.

The authorities won't find your island for you, and won't sell it to you until you have seen it. But once you have picked it out, they will make you one of the best propositions you will find anywhere. If your island is ten acres in area or less, you can have the whole thing for forty-five dollars an acre. If the island you pick is more than ten acres, you can buy up to ten acres of it (you can buy just one acre or even less if that's all you want) for the same price.

There are plenty of ten-acre-or-less islands, and many island owners say that this is by far the best size range. In case you are a city dweller and have difficulty visualizing acreages, a ten-acre island if perfectly square would be 220 yards on each side. That's more than four average city blocks. A square five-acre island would be about 155 yards on each side.

There's one condition of sale. If you intend the island for the use of yourself, your family and your friends only, and if it is five acres in area or less, you must build some kind of shelter worth at least five hundred dollars within eighteen

months of the date of your purchase. If you buy a bigger
island, you must undertake to increase the value of your
building by five hundred dollars for each acre over five. That
adds up to a minimum of three thousand dollars in buildings
for a ten-acre, maximum-size island. Since you would probably find it impossible to build any kind of cottage for less
than five hundred dollars, and since you don't have to take
more than five acres unless you want to, this condition is no
drawback. If you wish, you can build a cabin yourself, as
many have done, and count your own time in reaching the
five-hundred-dollar valuation figure. You'll get help in this
from the local District Forester, who will help you select
the best building site on the island and advise you on construction methods. He will also tell you which trees you can cut and
which you can't, for the provincial government wisely retains
the right to supervise all timber on crown lands which it sells.

You will encounter one other small expense, something like
the title search fee involved in buying a house in the United
States. If the island already has been surveyed, you must pay
a forty-dollar survey charge at the time you make application to buy it. If it hasn't been surveyed, you can pay eighty
dollars and it will be surveyed for you. Or if you have the
time to spare, an Ontario land surveyor can make it at your
direction and expense, which probably will come to considerably less than eighty dollars.

All the foregoing applies if you intend the island for your
private use only. If you want to take in paying guests, the
conditions are slightly different. If the island you choose is
ten acres or less in area, you must erect buildings to a value
of at least two thousand dollars. You can take larger parcels
for this purpose, though, up to a maximum of twenty acres.
For each additional acre over ten you have to spend another
two thousand dollars in buildings, up to a maximum of

twenty-two thousand dollars for a twenty-acre parcel. Several Americans have established such resorts in Ontario, mostly for hunting and fishing purposes. Some have been quite successful, and a few were utter failures.

(Some of these charges probably will be raised in the near future, though they had not been as of November, 1952. Most likely to be raised, according to provincial officials, is the minimum requirement of five hundred dollars in improvements. Survey charges probably will be a little higher too.)

There is one other possibility. If you want to go whole hog and retire to an island permanently, you can homestead on one in Ontario. In order to do this you have to become a Canadian citizen, or at least indicate your intention of becoming naturalized as soon as you are eligible. You also have to be "a male of at least eighteen years of age, or a female who is the sole head of a family with a child or children under eighteen years of age residing with her."

For those who can satisfy these conditions, there are several hundred thousand acres of arable Crown lands still available for homesteading. Most of it is in the northern half of the province, and a good deal of it is on lake islands. You would need a determined pioneering spirit but very little cash. The purchase price is only fifty cents per acre, and if you served in His Majesty's Active Force outside of Canada during either the first or second World Wars, you don't have to pay even this.

Depending on the area, you can take up from 80 to 320 acres to start with and add more later. At least half the land must be proven arable. After you make your application, you must reside on the land for at least six months of each of three consecutive years and must build a habitable dwelling at least sixteen feet by twenty feet in size. You must also bring from ten to twenty per cent of the island under cultivation, depending on its size. Once you have satisfied all these conditions, the island is yours. And you will really have earned it, the hardest way possible.

If you are not yet sure that you want to buy an Ontario island and would prefer to give it a try first, the provincial government will help you with this, too. You can rent an island up to five acres in area for ten dollars per acre per year. You can either camp out on it or build a rough cabin. If you could enjoy a back-to-nature type of vacation, this obviously is an excellent way to learn the facts of island life.

With so many islands and such varied possibilities to choose among, the chief question is where to start looking. Unless you live west of Chicago, in which case you probably will be more interested in the far western islands of Ontario (see Chapter IX), the best place to begin is Georgian Bay. Its islands include the Thirty Thousand Island group, which hugs the northeastern shore of the bay, plus several dozen others along the coast of Bruce Peninsula, which forms the bay's southwestern shore. Most of the latter are now privately owned. But of the twenty-two thousand islands which have been surveyed in the Thirty Thousand group, only five thousand have been taken up. The other seventeen thousand plus all those unsurveyed are Crown lands and, except for a few set aside as provincial parks, are for sale or rent under the terms I have described.

Among the places from which you might start exploring them are Owen Sound, Midland, Parry Sound and Pointe au Baril. All are within two or three hundred miles of Detroit or Buffalo, and you can easily find a good route on any road map of the province. There also are a number of ways to reach the Georgian Bay area via steamers across Lake Huron. Service varies from year to year, but you can find out about it at Detroit, Port Huron or Sault Ste. Marie (all in Michigan). From the east a lake steamer trip would be a roundabout route through Lake Erie, Lake St. Clair and on into Lake Huron, but if you want to take the extra time, you can find out about the service at Buffalo.

At Owen Sound you can take a lake steamer for either a week-end or a five-day cruise among the Georgian Bay islands. And from Tobermory at the tip of Bruce Peninsula there is a regular car ferry service to Manitoulin Island, which is the world's largest fresh-water-lake island and which forms the northwestern shore of Georgian Bay. But if you are reasonably agile and experienced at camping out, you may find it much more enjoyable to hire a motorboat or a canoe, with or without a guide, at Midland or Parry Sound and set out on your own along the route of the early French *voyageurs*.

This is not nearly so difficult an undertaking as it may sound. Several of the local tourist travel groups with the provincial authorities' help have organized to chart and mark the canoe routes of Samuel de Champlain and the other explorers of the area. It was Champlain who, three and a half centuries ago, named the Bay the Mer Douce, Gentle Sea, and it still deserves the name. Even if one of the rare storms should blow up, you will always find an island shelter near at hand. Camps for latter-day *voyageurs* have been set up on many of the islands all along the route. You can spend a few days or, if you like, the whole summer drifting around among the islands, putting into port only occasionally for supplies. Alternatively, you can put into one or another of the numerous island resorts which vary from simple and cheap tent camps to luxurious and expensive lodges, from a couple of dollars to thirty dollars or more per day.

You can also take some of your supplies from the water. Lake trout, pickerel, large-mouth and black bass, pike and muskellunge (known locally as maskinonge) are plentiful. Fishing licenses for visitors are $5.50 per person or $8 for a family.

You can also drive on past Parry Sound and approach the islands from the north at Pointe au Baril (pronounced "point oh barrel"). The Pointe is principally a supply base for island owners who spend summers on their islands nearby, and the village consists chiefly of storage for cars, general store, grocery, docks for commercial boats and water taxis and waterside gasoline stations. Within a few miles south or west or north are hundreds of pleasant little islands. Many of those nearest the mainland have been taken up, but there still remain plenty of others farther out.

You may not find it easy to meet the islanders and talk over island owning with them, unless you know someone who owns an island there and who will formally introduce you. Many of the old-timers resent newcomers.

"We first came up here forty-two years ago," one man from Washington, D. C., told me, "and most of my family has spent every summer here since. When we bought our island, motorboats were practically unknown. There was no telephone nor even horse-drawn transportation within forty miles of the Pointe. Mail reached us only twice a week. We could hear wolves way off in the timber, and occasionally we saw bears on the mainland. When we arrived here every June, we really got back to nature.

"Then more and more people began coming up, and they dragged civilization in with them. The silence of our night is torn with the sounds of speedboats and outboards. Fishermen come up and troll for pike and muskellunge with an outboard motor instead of in the time-honored way of the water — by rowboat and oars. I suppose we are selfish and have no moral justification, but we want to hold on to as much as possible of our seclusion and the beauty of this part of the country."

This, of course, is the cry of the old-timer in the backwoods everywhere. And it is somewhat exaggerated, for there are many islanders who have little trouble holding civilization at bay. Being one of the early arrivals, the family in question took up one of the islands close to the shore. But there are plenty of others farther out, where the passing of a fisherman so improper as to troll from an outboard would be a rarity. Few of the islanders can afford or see any sense in the expense of an underwater cable to provide telephone service, and the highway and railroad to Pointe au Baril make it possible to reach your island quickly instead of spending several days on the trip and to bring in supplies.

It would take a far bigger invasion by civilization than seems even remotely in prospect to destroy the beauty of the area. The islands are part of the great Laurentian shield, earth's oldest geological formation, a broad, low plateau of ancient rock which covers most of Ontario. Many of the islands have huge, bare granite outcroppings streaked with rose feldspar and white quartz. Most also have plentiful stands of pine and cedar. The floor of the bay which separates them is unencumbered with weeds and the water unclouded.

Indeed, the water is so clear and so pure nearly everywhere in the Ontario island areas that the drinking and bathing water problem which besets owners of sea islands is nonexistent. You simply run a pipe a little way out under the water from some point on your shore and pump all you need to your cottage. A septic tank for your sewage will keep the surrounding water permanently pure.

As for swimming, the water of Georgian Bay and of nearly all Canadian lakes is fine — if you like it cold. Even in July and August it keeps you moving as long as you remain in it.

But those who like it swear by it. They indulge in a sport called island-hopping — swimming from island to island and trying to get back where they started by a route different from that by which they left.

One Georgian Bay island owner has remarkable facilities for another sport. When he bought the island, he looked around for a likely spot on which to build a tennis court. He found one on which the only construction activity necessary was drilling holes for the net posts. It is a solid sheet of granite slightly larger than court size and as smooth and level as freshly poured concrete. Although he and his family have played on it for years, they haven't yet marred it with a single chip.

You may not be able to find anything quite like this among the twenty-five thousand or so Georgian Bay islands still available for sale by the provincial government, but there still is plenty of choice. And one of the best things about the area is that there are many contractors who have experience in, and some who specialize in, building island homes. Even for your minimum five hundred dollars you can, if you are willing to do a lot of the work yourself and can round up a few friends to help you, put up at least a modest cottage. And, old-timers to the contrary notwithstanding, the availability of water taxis and grocery delivery service near Pointe au Baril, Parry Sound and Midland can be a big help.

Occasionally some of the five thousand islands already taken up are offered for sale by their private owners, and you can pick up an island complete with house, dock and plumbing facilities. One was offered not long ago by a Pittsburgh man and a New York woman, brother and sister, who owned it jointly. Located between Pointe au Baril and about seven miles off the mainland, it is a little under an acre and well wooded. There are four cottages with sleeping accommodations for seven to ten people which are offered complete with furnishings, bedding, utensils and kitchen equipment. Two good docks, two square-stern boats and an outboard motor also are included. The asking price, at last report, was $7500.

At the opposite extreme from this civilized sort of island are those farther north along the eastern shore of the bay. Several at the mouth of the French River, some thirty miles north of Pointe au Baril, will take you well beyond the reach of any grocery or other service. A group of Louisville, Kentucky, physicians and lawyers has found an excellent use for one of these islands. They organized themselves as a club, bought the island under the "resort islands" regulations and built a small lodge on it. Every summer they charter a plane in Louisville and fly up to the island for two weeks of complete escape from all patients and clients.

"They prescribe complete rest for each other," a man who was once a guest on the island told me, "and they make sure that the prescription is taken literally — washed down, of course, with good, sour-mash bourbon."

One way of taking the prescribed rest is an unusual kind of fishing. The water of the French River estuary is crystal-clear, and the rocky bottom is twelve to fifteen feet deep almost everywhere. Instead of fishing at random, you can paddle quietly along in a canoe until you spot a likely-looking fish, then start casting. Restful, hour-long battles with five-pound bass are standard features of the cure.

Further north and west along the northern shore of Lake Huron civilization reasserts itself to some extent among the islands of the North Channel. This is another arm of Lake Huron cut off from the main body of the lake to the south and from Georgian Bay to the east by the huge, seventy-five-mile bulk of Manitoulin Island. You can reach the North Channel by steamer across the lake or by highways from the east, but the latter take a several-hundred-mile detour to the north before they reach the Channel. The Channel's islands probably will appeal more to Midwesterners who can drive there via Sault Ste. Marie, which is within easy reach of most Midwestern cities.

Manitoulin Island itself is so big that it scarcely seems like an island, since you cannot see from any point on it that you are completely surrounded by water. In any case most of it already is taken up in farms and Indian reservations. However, from Manitoulin towns such as Meldrum Bay on the west, Gore Bay in the center and Little Current on the east, all of which can be reached via automobile ferries, you can set out to explore the smaller islands of the Channel. Or you can start out from Thessalon, Blind River or Algoma on the mainland northern shore of the Channel.

As is usually the case with island groups, no one seems to have counted those in the North Channel. But there are at least several hundred still owned by the provincial government and available for sale under its terms. Two of the chief concentrations are in McGregor Bay and Bay of Islands at the eastern end of North Channel. You can rent a motorboat, with or without guide, at Little Current and spend from a day to a whole summer exploring them.

Another much faster way to reconnoiter would be by plane, and you can charter small seaplanes for that purpose in the area. One such charter-plane service charges twenty-four dollars per person for flying in a six-passenger plane to fishing camps on small lakes to the north and probably would want at least a three-figure fee for a day of island exploration. But you could make a brief and cheaper flight over the islands, pick the ones that look best to you from the air, then return by motorboat for a closer look.

Some of the towns in the North Channel area also have

private surveying services. These are devoted mostly to commercial purposes such as locating timber lands, establishing mining claims and such. But at least one of them — Algoma Lands & Surveys in Sault Ste. Marie — will help you locate an island and negotiate its purchase.

One Wisconsin family I know has been spending summers on a North Channel island for many years. Now the children — two daughters and a son — have married and started families of their own. Each of them has spent one summer away from the island with his or her spouse.

"And," one of the daughters told me, "it was like wandering in the wilderness. I hardly knew what to do with myself. Once you're used to the complete freedom and complete privacy of vacationing on your own island, you hardly know how to enjoy yourself somewhere else."

All three of the younger generation's spouses eventually came around to the same way of thinking. Now each of the families has claimed or is planning to claim an island near the original one. They may, they think, have started a family tradition. Perhaps their children will some day take up other islands nearby too, then their children's children and so on until they run out of islands, but that eventuality is many generations distant.

So much for the Ontario islands of the Great Lakes. Although they are among the most accessible, they are by no means the only ones of interest. There are thousands of others available on the same terms, and easy to reach from many parts of the United States, in the countless smaller lakes of southern and eastern Ontario. And "smaller" is strictly a term to describe them in comparison with the Great Lakes. Some of them cover thousands of square miles and offer thousands of islands.

In the most southerly and populous part of the province

most of the islands have been taken up, and buying or renting one would be a matter for negotiation with the private owner. But within only a few hours' drive from Toronto you still can find islands which are Crown lands. You also can find proof that the countryside is far from overcivilized.

A couple of years ago a Pennsylvania man was driving toward Toronto from Cobourg, some sixty miles east along the shore of Lake Ontario. A huge "dog" leaped out of the forest lining the road, right into the path of his car. It was killed instantly. He tied the carcass to a fender and drove to the nearest farmhouse to apologize. Instead of reproaches, he was met with the news that he had earned fifty dollars in bounties. The "dog" was a timber wolf.

One good way to explore some of the nearest and best of these smaller lakes and their islands is by a motorboat or sailboat cruise through the Trent Canal system and the Kawartha chain of lakes. Starting at Trenton on Lake Ontario's Bay of Quinte and winding up on Georgian Bay, this is a prehistoric Indian canoe route paralleled by the Iroquois Trail. But instead of portaging around falls and rapids, you can now negotiate the whole distance afloat with the help of a system of locks. Some of the route is through farm land, but much of it is through wild country replete with fish and game. And hundreds of islands are scattered over the dozen-odd lakes through which you pass. (You can get navigation charts for the system from the Superintending Engineer, Trent Canal, Peterborough, Ontaria.)

A Toronto owner of one of these islands is the fortunate recipient of an annual six-week vacation. He usually sails out of Toronto early in July and takes a leisurely week to reach his island. He spends a month there, occasionally cruising farther along the canal system. Toward the end of August he closes his cottage and sails back to reality, "so relaxed," he told a friend of mine, "in body, mind and soul that it takes me several months to remember what it's like to feel jittery."

Another island deep in the system — big Boyd Island in Pigeon Lake — once was put to a use for which islands are ideal by nature, an experiment in animal crossbreeding. On an island you can simply turn loose opposite sexes of the animals you want to cross and let nature take its course. You don't have to guard against intruders from some other range.

In this case the purpose was to cross American buffaloes with beef cattle to produce an animal hardy enough to winter out in a severe northern climate. The cross was easily achieved, and the result, a fine animal which produced good meat, was named a "catalo." But unfortunately the catalo proved to be sterile, like the mule, and the experiment ended in disillusionment for its perpetrators.

There's also a case of a disappearing island in one of the lakes of the Trent Canal system. Once known as Steamboat Island because of its shape, it is now marked only by a few dying trees which barely show their tops above water. Such disappearances are extremely rare in Ontario lakes, however, and you need have no fear that it will happen to your island. This one occurrence is neatly explained in a local legend.

The tale is credited to an Indian guide. He made camp for a party of his fishing clients one evening on an island not far from the remains of Steamboat. Over their postprandial campfire the fishermen got to telling the usual fanciful tales of the big ones which had gotten away. The guide joined the competition.

Trolling near Steamboat Island one morning, he told them, he had hooked an enormous muskellunge. It proved so powerful that it began dragging his boat down the lake. Not wanting to spend the day rowing back from the opposite end, he maneuvered toward Steamboat, leaped ashore and made several turns around the island with his line. Leaving the fish tied to the island, he rowed off to get help. When he returned, the muscular muskie had dragged the whole island into the depths of the lake, leaving only a few trees showing.

Near the western end of the Trent Canal system lie the Muskoka Lakes — Rosseau, Joseph and Muskoka. There are well over one thousand islands scattered among them, but almost all of these now are privately owned. They were discovered half a century ago by the tycoon crowd. Off the village of Beaumaris on the eastern shore of Lake Muskoka, for instance, lies a chain of islands known locally and literally as "Millionaires' Row," where Andrew Mellon and other Pittsburghers built thirty-room summer shacks in the good old days of bad big business.

Naturally, the modern tax rates have taken their toll here as in other plush summering areas. Most of the island owners in this area, however, manage to keep up quite impressive appearances. There also are several luxurious and expensive resort hotels such as Royal Muskoka and Wigwassan Lodge on islands in Lake Rosseau. And just twenty miles further east is the Lake of Bays, where Bigwin Inn on Bigwin Island is said to be the most luxurious resort hotel in Ontario.

You will find plenty of other far less expensive stopping places, however, on islands in this area. Some offer cottages with full housekeeping facilities for as little as twenty-five or thirty dollars a week, a sum which would just about buy you a room with bath for a single night at the big-name places. And occasionally there are bargain tax sales of private island homes. There is a Tax Sale Service organization in Toronto (listed among the further information sources at the end of the chapter) which will keep you informed of these opportunities.

Further north, in Algonquin Provincial Park, are hundreds of small lakes rich in Crown lands islands. These come under the authority of the park administration and are not available for sale, but you can take one on a long-term lease. The maximum size you can take is two acres, and the rent is fifteen dollars per year per acre. And, as in buying islands elsewhere in the province, you must contract to put up a cottage worth five hundred dollars within eighteen months. You can also lease islands up to five acres for commercial purposes in the park, and the annual rent is only twenty dollars per acre per year.

If you want to venture still farther north, your range of choice becomes almost unlimited. Within a hundred and fifty miles of the Muskoka Lakes region (altogether about four hundred miles from Buffalo and five hundred miles from Detroit) along highways which are not always hard-surfaced but which are well-built, you will find tens of thousands of lakes. Nearly all have at least a few islands. One of them, Lake Temagami, has 12,079 surveyed islands. All but 670 of these still are Crown lands available on the usual terms. On the lake there are several resorts, ranging from imposing lodges to mere tenting grounds, which you can use for bases from which to explore. The town of Temagami offers storage for your car, all sorts of boats for rent, everything you will need for outfitting your expedition, agents who will help you close the deal on your island and builders experienced in putting up island homes. If you don't want to drive, the Ontario Northland Railway provides good service to the town of Temagami and operates several boat lines around the lake. (Incidentally, there seems to be some confusion about how the name of the lake and town should be spelled, so don't be confused if you see it written "Timagami.")

Lake Nipissing offers almost as much as Temagami. Your

best base for exploring it probably would be the town of North Bay, near the eastern end, although you could start from Cache Bay at the western end. Most of the smaller lakes in the region would take you well out of reach of the services available in these two big ones.

If you go much farther north than the Lake Temagami area, you will be entirely on your own. Highways and railroads do penetrate the region, but venturing a mile or two away from them can take you into complete wilderness. Indeed, the Ontario Northland Railway goes all the way to Moosonee on Hudson Bay. For information about any islands there, you will have to go to the Eskimos.

## Sources of Additional Information

GENERAL
    Canadian Government Travel Bureau
    Department of Resources and Development
    Ottawa, Canada

QUEBEC
  *General*
    Tourist Branch
    Provincial Publicity Bureau
    Quebec, Province of Quebec, Canada

  *Real-Estate Dealer*
    Previews, Inc.
    49 East 53rd Street
    New York 22, N. Y.

ONTARIO
  *General*
      For any further information about the province's Crown lands
      policies:

Division of Land and Recreational Areas
Department of Lands and Forests
Parliament Buildings
Toronto, Ontario, Canada

For information about traveling facilities in the province:
Department of Travel and Publicity
Parliament Buildings
Toronto, Ontario, Canada

> (Among the most useful things you can request are: "Ontario Road Map," "Where to Stay in Ontario," "The Fisherman's Ontario," and "Flying Facts About Ontario.")

For further information about individual areas (the procedure once you find an island you want is to make application through the District Forester), write to *District Forester, Department of Lands and Forests,* at any of the following addresses, all of which are in *Ontario, Canada:*

Chapleau Area: Chapleau
Cochrane Area: Cochrane
Gogama Area: Gogama
Kapuskasing Area: Kapuskasing
North Bay Area: North Bay
Quinte Area: Tweed
Sault Ste. Marie Area: Sault Ste. Marie
Sudbury Area: Sudbury
Trent Area: Lindsay
> (Local Forest Rangers also can sometimes help you find your island by telling you where to look for what types.)

Canadian railroads want to promote American tourist travel and maintain good information services. Here are three which can be particularly helpful about lake islands in the areas through which they pass:

General Tourist Office
Canadian Pacific Railway
Dominion Square Building
Montreal, Quebec, Canada

Ontario Northland Railway
North Bay
Ontario, Canada

C. A. Rowe
Superintendent of Lands and Forests
Algoma Central Railway
Sault Ste. Marie, Ontario, Canada

A few of Ontario's private business associations are island-conscious. Here are three which can be helpful in their own areas:

Blind River Chamber of Commerce
Blind River
Ontario, Canada

Chamber of Commerce
10 Brock Street
Sault Ste. Marie, Ontario, Canada

Bruce Peninsula Resort Association
Wiarton
Ontario, Canada

At Algonquin Provincial Park the man to see is:

Park Superintendent
Algonquin Park P. O.
Ontario, Canada

*Real-Estate Dealers*
Among those who have handled island properties in their areas are:

William R. Chitty
495 Queen Street E.
Sault Ste. Marie, Ontario, Canada

E. Bruce Fleming
356 Queen Street E.
Sault Ste. Marie, Ontario, Canada

E. E. Bennett
Real Estate Broker
Wiarton, Ontario, Canada

Locating service:
Algoma Lands and Surveys
Locating Service
175 Queen Street E.
Sault Ste. Marie, Ontario, Canada

For island tax sales:
Tax Sale Service
120 Bloor Street West
Toronto, Ontario, Canada

CHAPTER IV

## Coastal Islands of New England

Not long ago a young New York college professor was strolling down a narrow village street in Falmouth, Massachusetts, near the southern end of Cape Cod. A photograph in a real-estate agent's window caught her eye. It was labeled "Island For Sale — $3000." Within only a few hours the island was hers.

Located in a pond which connects with the sea via a tidal creek, it is less than an acre in size, but to her every square inch is nearly perfect. She can dig clams or trap crabs at will anywhere around it. Only a few minutes away by motorboat is a long stretch of Nantucket Sound beach too far out of the way for the usual Cape Cod crowds. And her nearest mainland neighbors are only faintly audible even in their loudest moments. It is altogether the island of her dreams.

It is also a fair example of the three-thousand-odd islands which lie scattered along the coast of New England from the northern tip of Maine to Rhode Island. Unlike the Canadian islands, few of these are held by the Federal or state governments, and those few are not available either for sale or rent except in extremely rare instances. Almost every year, however, a number of the privately owned islands are offered for sale, and homes or camp sites on hundreds of others are rented every year for periods ranging from a week end to several years. Substantial homes or, at least, good livable cottages have been built on most of the islands, but there still remain a considerable number encumbered with nothing but wild growths of pine, spruce and oak. The latter of course are much the cheapest, and a few of them can be picked up for as little as two or three hundred dollars.

This chapter covers the islands off the coasts of Maine, New Hampshire, Massachusetts and Rhode Island, leaving Connecticut until later. Because all its coastal islands are in Long Island Sound and because most of its more interesting ones are within easy reach of New York City — a geographical fact which the prices clearly reflect — I think they belong in Chapter VII on the islands of coastal New York.

## Maine

As a truly straightforward, single-minded crow would fly it, Maine's coastline is only 250 miles long. But bays, inlets and islands are so numerous and so irregular in their formation that they give the state a total tidal shoreline of more than 2500 miles. Much of that shoreline, both on the mainland and on the islands, consists of great granite cliffs which are either stark and forbidding or magnificently inspiring, depending on how you look at them. But there are also hundreds of miles of comfortable sandy beaches scattered among the various islands.

Maine's boosters like to call the state "Vacationland" and work hard to earn the name. The state now attracts more than a million visitors a year, mostly during the summer. Since its permanent population is only a little over nine hundred thousand, this huge influx makes for considerable crowding of accommodations in the more popular resort areas. As a result many Maine vacationers who don't like crowds are turning to the islands to escape being hemmed in, and this seems bound to push up the prices of island homes. But you can still find many good buys of improved islands in the five-thousand-and-under class.

As usual, there has been no authoritative count of the islands along Maine's coast, but one estimate is that there are approximately twenty-five hundred in the habitable class. Only eight of them are ten square miles or larger in size. One of these is 108-square-mile Mount Desert Island, part of which has been set aside as Acadia National Park and part of which makes up the now slightly decaying but once superswank Bar Harbor enclave. Some of the other large ones, such as Vinalhaven in Penobscot Bay, are so broken up by coves and inlets that they seem more like several small islands than one big one, and a home on one of the many points will give you almost as much privacy as a completely separate island. But there are also plenty of small, one-family types to choose from.

Like much of the rest of the state, Maine's islands are devoted mostly to the summer vacationing of escapees from the heat waves further south. And many of the islands are pollen-free havens for hay fever victims. If you hope to make your island your permanent home and the source of your income, your best bet will be taking in such paying guests during the summer and fall. During the rest of the year your life alone on your island will be much like life on old-time sailing ships on the long passage around the Horn and out to the Far East. Most of your activities will depend on the moods of the wind and the sea. Occasionally, those two elements will get into a fury and either exhilarate you or scare you half out of your wits by trying to batter the island to pieces.

It will take a good deal of ingenuity or luck to find a way of making a living out of a Maine island other than out of paying guests. Few of the islands have much arable land. And don't fall to dreaming of a life of island ease earned by a daily catch of a few of those Maine lobsters which you have seen sold for three dollars apiece or more in your local restaurants. You have to be a Maine resident for ten years to be eligible for a lobster license, and the competition is expert and incessant. You can get a commercial clam-digging license more easily, but there is nothing easy about digging the clams.

One World War II veteran who bought a Maine island, however, did find a neat way of making a living off it. He bought a small plane and equipped it with pontoons. Using the island as a base, he flies out to sea seeking schools of fish, some types of which are plainly visible from the air. When he has found a big school and has determined the direction and speed in which it is moving, he heads for shore and guides a group of commercial fishing boats out to the fish. His percentage of the proceeds gives him a good income.

Ideas as bright as this, however, are extremely rare. But if all you want of your island is peace and quiet, that is easy to come by along the Maine coast. Two more points ought to be considered, though, before we get down to the islands themselves.

First is your transportation to and from your island. In Casco Bay, in Penobscot Bay and in the area around Mount Desert Island you could, perhaps, depend entirely on water taxi service and on the delivery services of local grocers. But even in these localities you probably would want some sort of boat in order to avoid such complete dependence, and elsewhere a boat would be a must. Fortunately, Maine has numerous small-boat builders. You can have an eighteen-foot combination sailboat and outboard motorboat, hull only, made to order for about three hundred dollars. Decking at the bow, sails and rigging and a new outboard motor would bring the total cost to about a thousand. But a little shopping might turn up a secondhand equivalent of this for five hundred or less. Such a boat, if you are reasonably good at handling it, would be quite safe for getting to and from most Maine islands in fair summer weather. A boat for reaching islands well out to sea and in less calm weather probably would cost several times this amount, and you would have to be an expert sailor.

The second consideration is drinking water. If you are buying an island already equipped with a well, you ought to make quite sure that it is dependable. If possible, get a guarantee in writing. Buying one without a well means taking a big risk. One Maine well driller who works on islands charges five to six dollars per foot and makes absolutely no promise of results. Since fresh water floats on salt water, there is always a chance that you will find it at a reasonable depth, but if you are unlucky, you will suffer deep in your purse.

There are several different ways to go about exploring the Maine islands. One is to drive along the coast on U. S. Highway #1, taking occasional seaward detours on local roads when the through highway bends inland. You will find magnificent vistas of the islands from high coastal headlands. And when you find a group that looks especially interesting, you can rent a sailboat or a motorboat for a closer look. In some places local real-estate dealers will sail you out to the islands.

Another way is to sail along the coast in your own or a rented boat. There are inns or camping places where you can stop over on a number of the islands. Out of Portland and some of the other towns there are summer vacation cruises among the islands. One type of cruise is on a sailing schooner, and the passengers join in the more glamorous parts of the work of the crew, hauling up the sails, taking reefs in them and winding the windlass with much chanting of sea chanteys.

You can find islands scattered all the way to Eastport on Moose Island in Passamaquoddy Bay, whose boosters like to point out that it is the most easterly city in the United States. Among the best jumping-off points in the eastern region of the state are Machiasport for the islands of Machias Bay, Jonesport for the islands of Channel Bay, Millbridge for the islands of Pleasant Bay, and Bar Harbor or Seal Harbor for the islands of French, Bluehill and Western Bays.

One island in Western Bay was advertised some time ago under the billing "Kingdom for Sale," and it deserves the billing. Four miles long and three miles wide and about half a mile off the mainland, it has twenty miles of shoreline which varies from overhanging cliffs to sandy coves. About half of it is in hardwood and spruce forest, half in pasture land. The buildings include a main house of twelve rooms with three baths and automatic heat, a nine-room caretaker's house with bath and heat, and two guest cottages, one of which dates back to Revolutionary War days. In addition, there are a barn, cowshed, garage, blacksmith shop, henhouse, smokehouse, slaughterhouse, wagon shed, shingle mill, portable sawmill and farm equipment, plus a boathouse, pier and small boat.

And that is still not all. Clams are plentiful around the shore, and fishing good in the water. Dozens of deer roam the woods. A duck pond attracts waterfowl the year round, and thousands of ducks and geese turn up every fall. Partridge and pheasant dote on the place.

It is obviously the sort of island to which you could retire and forget completely about the rest of the world. But it's equally obvious that paying for it would do severe damage to the bank account of even a millionaire.

On the other hand there are in the same area dozens of other island homes well within the reach of families who can budget only a few hundred dollars per year for their summer vacations. For that matter, a family whose members enjoy camping out can have a couple of weeks on Mount Desert Island for little more than the cost of the gas and oil necessary to reach it. Clams, fish, and wild blueberries are so plentiful in some seasons that you can almost live off the land.

Don't let the name of the island fool you. There is nothing the least bit desertlike about it. According to one story of how it got its odd name, a group of early surveyors of the island anchored off it late one evening and were much impressed by the view of a tree-clad mountain in its center. They decided to wait until morning to start the survey. But during the night a fog blew in, so that the mountain had disappeared from view by morning. They called it Mount Desert because it had deserted them, and the name later was applied to the whole island.

Actually, much of the island is covered with pine and spruce forest which extends in many places right down to the sea. Some of the hills rise steeply more than fifteen hundred feet out of the sea, and Somes Sound, which cuts the island nearly in two, is a steep-walled replica of a Norwegian fjord.

Much of the most beautiful scenery of the island is included in Acadia National Park, where there are numerous free camping sites. In the privately owned parts of the island your choice of living accommodations varies from motels to summer cottages at fifty dollars or so per month to luxurious hotels where you can easily spend fifty dollars a day. But since the forest fire of a couple of years back, which temporarily destroyed much of the beauty of the Bar Harbor end of the island, the latter sort of thing has been fading. Many of the

Bar Harbor mansion owners were delighted to collect their insurance and be rid of their white elephants.

Because of its size, the number of tourists it attracts and its connection to the mainland by a bridge, Mount Desert is not what most people have in mind in the way of islands. It is the dozens of smaller islands in the waters around Mount Desert that are the real thing. And if you would like to get an introductory taste of life on a small sea island, any of several of them would be a fine place for it. They offer for rent anything from a small cottage to an imposing mansion for any period from a couple of weeks to a whole summer.

A few years ago a New York newspaperman I know spent his annual month of July vacation with his family at a mainland resort farther south down the Maine coast. One day they drove to Mount Desert Island to see the park. From a hilltop there they glimpsed a group of half a dozen small green islands offshore.

"All of us," he tells the story, "decided then and there that any of those islands would be the perfect place to spend our vacations. But we also decided that we would never get the chance. For some reason we just assumed that a private island, or even a semiprivate island, was something that only a wealthy family could afford.

"Well, we wanted to stay overnight on Mount Desert, so we had dinner in a pleasant little restaurant overlooking those islands. After we had ordered, we sat staring out at the islands sort of wistfully. While we watched, a small sailboat put out from one of them, sailed straight toward us and docked right under our noses. A middle-aged couple got out and came into the restaurant.

"Maybe it was the fact that they had sailed the boat in themselves instead of having some kind of boat-chauffeur bring them in. Anyway, the sight of them gave me hope. I went over to their table, introduced myself and explained that my family and I had been admiring the islands and wondering whether there was any chance of renting a summer place on any of them.

" 'Why, yes,' the fellow told me, 'there are two of them for rent on ours. I think they are asking about a hundred a month. But there's a real-estate agent down the way who can tell you all about it.'

"I was at the agent's office when he opened the next morning. He took us straight out to the island, and we rented one of the cottages for the rest of the month even though we had already paid a month's rent on the place where we had been staying. That afternoon we drove down to pick up our things and got back and settled on our island by night. We have been going back to it every summer since."

As were many of the islanders I talked to, he was worried about the effect on his privacy of any publicity, and I had to promise not to be too specific about the location of his island. I can say, though, that it is of the semiprivate type with about twenty houses scattered around its perimeter. Few of the houses are within sight or sound of any of the others, and each has its own stretch of shoreline and usually its own dock. During the summers there are from a hundred to a hundred and fifty inhabitants, mostly professional, people who come from all over the country, including a few from as far away as California. The island's code of manners prohibits any invasion of privacy except on specific invitation. But most of its central portion is a sort of common domain, and there are frequent gatherings for clambakes and such on the beach. As it is along most of Maine's coast, the water is cold even in midsummer, and you have to be a devoted amphibian to enjoy swimming. A more favored sport is making day-long sailing excursions among the other islands scattered around the area.

"It's not the kind of place," my friend says, "for anyone who likes hot, lazy weather. It's something like the coast of Norway, and you have to have Viking inclinations to enjoy it. Some people return, as we do, year after year. But we have had guests who left shivering in horror after only a couple of days."

On some of the islands for rent in the neighborhood you are also likely to encounter the more crotchety aspects of the Yankee character in your landlord. One novice in such matters rented an island on which there was a heavy growth of wild blueberries. He and his family were out picking berries one morning when the landlord hove to offshore and began berating them via a megaphone. He had rented to them, he said, only the use of the island and not of the blueberries. In another case a landlord insisted that renting his island did not include the right to use a natural spring on it.

The favorite story along this line, possibly apocryphal, is about a local owner whose island was pre-empted during the war for use as a Coast Guard station. The government built on it a watchtower and quarters for the crew manning it. At the end of the war the authorities prepared to dismantle these additions before returning the island. The owner quickly put a stop to that by claiming that he had given up only the right to build on the island and not the land itself. He forced the return of not only the island but also the buildings, intact.

About fifteen miles by sea south and west of Mount Desert Island you enter Penobscot Bay, an area rich in islands ranging from twenty-square-mile Vinalhaven down to little one-acre-or-less dots on the map. You can explore it from Rockland or Camden or Belfast on the western shore of the bay or from the towns of Deer Isle or Stonington on Deer Island, which is connected to the bay's eastern shore by a bridge. Or you can take a ferry from Rockland to the town of Vinalhaven on Vinalhaven Island and use it as your base. A little farther out the bay's name changes to Isle au Haut Bay, and there's a large island of the same name which is also connected with Rockland by ferry.

Some of the larger islands in the area are heavily settled and thoroughly civilized. Vinalhaven, for instance, is devoted mostly to big Victorian-mansion-style summer homes complete with wide verandas, cupolas, and widows' walks. A motor road system covers most of the island, and stores in the village provide delivery service to any part of it. You can even have a city-style plumbing system.

At the opposite extreme are a number of small islands inhabited only by birds, rabbits, squirrels, and other small wildlife. Although they are privately owned, the owners seem to take little interest in them. Picnickers use them frequently, and on some of them it is possible to camp out more or less indefinitely. Many years ago one of these islands was settled by a co-operative colony. It flourished until about the turn of the century. Then came the apparently inevitable quarrel and gradual disintegration. The last members left long ago, and now there aren't even any ruined houses to mark the place. Neighboring islanders have appropriated every stick of lumber.

Most of the owners of islands in this region spend only the summer on their property, and a few of them are glad to have someone live there free the rest of the year as caretakers. One impecunious writer I heard of found this the perfect solution of his housing problem a few years ago. For a couple of years he spent the summers traveling and returned to the island when the owners were ready to leave.

At least one escapee has found a way to make a success of year-round island life on the Maine coast. He is a young artist who, like most such, sells a painting only at rare intervals and for less than staggering prices. But by running a herring weir off his island home he has so far been able to eke out a modestly comfortable living and have plenty of time plus peace of mind for painting.

Another source of income for some island owners is sheep raising. A hundred-acre island in Penobscot Bay offered for sale some time ago included a hundred sheep in the deal. In addition, it had an eight-room house, a large barn and several smaller buildings, a well and a spring for drinking water and a natural harbor with a "good" depth of water. There were said to be good lobster grounds along the shore. But the asking price was twenty-five thousand dollars. You would have to run far more than a hundred sheep and work hard at it to make such an investment pay.

But this is by no means typical of the price asked for islands in the area. One real-estate dealer some time ago listed the following ten island properties in Penobscot and nearby Wheeler's and Muscongus Bays:

1. A sixteen-acre tract on a large island with a seven-room house and (for some odd reason) two cellars, one under the porch. There is a spring about fifty feet from the house. The acreage is in two separate plots, the house on one plot being set back a quarter of a mile from the shore. The other plot includes five hundred feet of shore-line. Annual taxes amount to about forty-five dollars. The asking price: $2000.

2. A complete fifty-acre island with a good sandy beach on the west shore and a stone beach on the east shore. In the center, between the beaches, the island is low and narrow. But the north and south ends are broader and rise at least forty feet above the sea, from which points the views over the sea and of the nearby islands are magnificent. Once a farm, the island now is grass-covered. Frost has damaged the well, and you would have to rebuild it. The asking price: $900.

3. An entire 350-acre island. It has a heavy stand of

wood, mostly spruce, which could be harvested for pulp. There is also grazing for sheep and a good water supply. A Coast Guard Life-saving Station occupies three quarters of an acre at one end of the island. The asking price: $10,000.

4. A one-acre portion of a seven-acre island owned and occupied by a single family. The island is connected to the mainland by a bridge. The acre consists of a narrow peninsula at one end of the island plus a rugged, spruce-covered bluff overlooking the peninsula. The asking price: $5000.

5. A 110-acre portion making up about one fourth of a large island. The shoreline is so broken that it stretches for nearly two miles. There is a good harbor with a stone wharf, a well and a stand of timber estimated at about a thousand cords of wood. The asking price: $7000.

6. A 190-foot shore frontage on a rugged little cottage-settled island connected to the mainland by a bridge. The frontage nestles in a spruce grove and has a two-room cabin equipped with electricity. Use of a community well goes with it. The asking price: $1500.

7. An entire island, about half a mile long and one eighth of a mile wide. A sixty-foot "peak" near its south shore gives a fine view out over Penobscot Bay. The asking price: $1100.

8. A one-acre shore plot on the south side of an eighty-acre island. About twenty acres of this island make up a Coast Guard Life-saving Station and lighthouse (the latter means that there would be the moaning of a foghorn to get used to in bad weather). There's no good landing on the plot for sale, but civilians always have been allowed to use the Coast Guard wharf. Most of the rest of the island is owned by a retired sea captain who has several good wells. You would have to get permission to use his or the Coast Guard's or drill your own. Most of the plot is on a ledge about forty feet above

the sea so that there is a fine view. It also has two hundred feet of shore line, a good stand of spruce and plenty of blueberries. The asking price: $200.

9. A rugged, rocky island one mile offshore. It has a shallow well in need of repair but which probably would be sufficient for drinking water only. Also, a granite wharf in fair condition. It is almost completely covered with spruce except for a granite quarry about fifty feet square and ten feet deep. The asking price: $1000.

10. An unnamed island about five miles out to sea from Port Clyde. Some 350 acres, it is covered with spruce. You might profitably sell half of it as pulpwood and still keep plenty standing. Cliffs at one end of the island tower a hundred feet above the sea and make a wonderful place from which to watch a storm, if you like that sort of thing. The island has two houses and a good well in use plus a spring which needs cleaning. In addition, there are one large cabin and four small ones which lobstermen rent as stopping places in case they are caught by a storm off the island or don't want to change their luck by returning to the mainland. The island's harbor is excellent. Taxes amount to a hundred dollars a year, but the lobstermen tenants provide an income of two or three times that amount. The asking price: $10,000.

By the time you read this, of course, it is possible that many or all of these offerings will have been sold. But they are typical of what is available, and other islands or parts of islands like these almost certainly will be for sale at much the same prices. Also, there are many other real-estate dealers along the Maine coast (you will find a list of several at the end of the chapter) who have island listings.

All the islands in the list of ten are fairly close inshore and can safely be reached in good weather by small boats. But

it is also possible here to cut all ties with the "main" and find
an island home so far out to sea that the shore is little more
than a shadow on the water. Matinicus, for instance, a seven-
hundred-acre island inhabited mostly by intensely independent
and intensively inbred fishermen, lies some fifteen miles from
shore at the nearest point. It is definitely not a resort island,
and you might not even be able to find a place to stay overnight. But if you would like to see what a "working" island
is like, there is a mailboat from Rockland on which you can
go out in the morning and return at the end of the day.

Fifteen miles to the east of Matinicus, and about ten miles
off the mainland, is Monhegan, an island of similar size which
specializes in summer boarders. But it is usually far from
crowded, and many of the visitors are amateur painters who
go in heavily for seascapes. You can reach Monhegan by scheduled steamers from Thomaston or Port Clyde, and there are
several inns with rates from around fifteen to fifty dollars
per week, the latter with meals.

At least three properties have been for sale there recently.
One is a seven-room cottage with a studio living room, bath
and fireplace. It is at the top of a steep bluff, has a magnificent
view over the sea and is said to be haunted. Offered furnished,
the latest asking price was $4500. Alternatively, you could
rent it for $150 a month. Another is a six-room house set in
a two-and-one-half-acre spruce grove with a well-kept garden
and an asking price of $8000. The third is an irregular plot
about a hundred by fifty-five feet set back a hundred yards
from the shore but with a good ocean view. It has only a
small cabin, and you would have to pipe water overground
from the town. But the asking price was only $1000.

Back inshore and a little farther down the coast I turned
up offers of two other island properties quite different from
any mentioned so far. One is a low, wooded island just a thou-

sand feet offshore near Popham Beach. About twelve acres in size, it offers, according to its owner, excellent duck hunting in season. There are no buildings on it. Its unusual feature is a sand bar which appears above the water at every low tide and for about an hour provides a bridge to the mainland. The asking price, said to be firm, was $3500.

The other oddity is an island with an old abandoned lighthouse which has been rebuilt as a year-round home. It was for sale at $7500 or for rent, with option to buy, at $1000 per year. If you have always dreamed of living in a lighthouse, this may be your one big chance, unless you want to join the United States Coast Guard. All coastal United States lighthouses are under the Coast Guard's jurisdiction, and the service no longer hires civilian lighthouse keepers but mans the lights with its own personnel.

Still farther south and west down the coast, nearing Portland, islands are quite numerous, but most of them are located in sheltered bays close inshore, are well built up and thoroughly civilized. Squirrel Island at the entrance to Boothbay Harbor, for instance, has boat service every half hour, and telephones, and is ringed by a concrete walk which is lighted for evening strollers. Like many other islands in this region it is governed by an association consisting of and financed by owners of property on the island.

Casco Bay, on which Portland is located, is another place which is supposed to have 365 islands, one for each day in the year. Actually, there are only 250 big enough even for names. They range from Pound of Tea, less than half an acre in size, to Sebascodegan, five miles long and about a mile wide. A few actually are suburbs, though an unusual type of suburb, of Portland. Peaks Island, which faces the harbor of Portland at a distance of about two miles, is only one square mile in area and has some twelve hundred houses. But many of these are summer cottages to which lucky Portlanders retire from June to September for rents which range as low as $250 per summer.

Several of the islands offered for sale at the end of World War II by the War Assets Administration were located in Casco Bay. Actually, none of them resembled even remotely the idyllic retreats which newspaper headlines at the time led many people to imagine they must be. One of these "islands for sale," for example, consisted of a small plot of ground on one of the most urbanized islands plus a steel lookout tower.

There are, however, dozens of islands in Casco Bay which do offer peace, quiet and an escape from too many neighbors. Most of these are owned by from one to a dozen families who use them chiefly as summer homes. Casco Bay Lines, based at Custom House Wharf in Portland, runs several excursion boat tours among the islands which provide a good way to inspect them if you are interested.

A good example of the old established community type of island is Birch Island, well up the bay from Portland toward the town of Brunswick. Unlike many islanders, Birch's owners are not at all reluctant to talk for publication about their summer retreat. One of them, Headmaster Walter F. Downey of Boston's English High School, described the island and his life there to me in great detail.

A little over one square mile in area, Birch has one year-round home, occupied by a family which looks after the island during the winter, and seventeen summer cottages. Many of the latter have been owned by the same families for three or four generations. Among them are teachers, preachers, lawyers, writers, artists and businessmen.

For half a century the island has been ruled by the Birch Island Improvement Association, patterned after a New England town meeting. It uses no constitution or set of bylaws but simply settles all problems of community interest by discussion and a majority vote. Through it the members tax themselves, and the taxes go to keep up a large floating wharf on the island and another at the mainland jumping-off point, a system of wells, a reservoir and water distribution pipes and similar community services.

"But," my informant says, "in modern improvements we have not many and we don't miss them. What need for electricity when a kerosene lamp provides excellent illumination? We want to live here as quietly and as peacefully as possible. Some of us, while living here, have seen two World Wars start, but world events have not changed the charm of the island, the rocks, the tides. Through the winter most of us dream of the summer and of return to the island."

Birch Island, obviously, is not a likely place to look for an island property for sale. Many of the other small Casco Bay islands are held by groups with similar close mutual interests of long standing. But others are less closely organized, and there are a few small, one-family islands. I did turn up one part-of-an-island which was on the block without community approval strings attached, though you probably would want to make sure you could get along with the other owners. This one consisted of a cottage surrounded by thirteen acres of beech, spruce and fir. Located on high ground overlooking the bay, it has a boat landing and float and was offered, with the cottage completely furnished, for five thousand dollars.

In spite of their general well-domesticated character, the islands of Casco Bay offer some out of the ordinary sights and experiences. Deep-sea fishing is one of them. And a couple of years ago three tuna fishermen who were working in the bay reported an experience which would be a thrill for the most blasé sportsman. Their thirty-seven-foot boat, they said, suddenly and without warning was hoisted high in the air on the back of a huge whale, then it slid gently and undamaged back into the water. Even if you wanted to, you probably would have difficulty hitching such a lift on a whale. But you can occasionally watch them surfacing and spouting among the islands, and groups of seals swim past now and then, too.

South and west of Portland along the Maine coast, islands become scarce. There are a dozen small ones in the Kennebunkport area, off Cape Porpoise. But this is one of the state's chief resort areas. Not far away is Old Orchard Beach, a five-mile stretch of white sand engulfed by some hundred and fifty hotels plus scores of rooming houses, restaurants and "amusement" concessions. So any island properties which might be offered probably would be at high prices.

In general, then, the farther north and east you go along the Maine coast the more numerous, the more rugged, the more available and the cheaper the islands you will find. If you don't want to go at least as far as the Portland area, you probably will do better to look elsewhere.

## New Hampshire

Although New Hampshire has only fifteen miles of coastline, its coast includes a group of several small islands known as the Isles of Shoals. They lie about seven miles off Portsmouth. Actually, the Maine–New Hampshire border splits the group, so that some of the islands are Maine territory, but Portsmouth is the best point from which to reach all of them.

A hundred years ago the Isles of Shoals were the home of an exceedingly Victorian poetess named Celia Thaxter, who made them famous by establishing a salon to which she lured such newsworthy figures as James Whitcomb Riley, John Greenleaf Whittier, violinist Ole Bull and President Franklin Pierce. Now the islands are strictly in the summer-home class, the only year-rounders, so I'm told, being the crew of the lighthouse on White Island and a few caretakers on the others. Star Island is owned by the Unitarian Conference Association and from June to September is the scene of a series of religious conferences. For contrast, one of the islands is named Smuttynose and was the scene of the famous Smuttynose murders.

Largest of the group is Appledore Island, about half-a-mile square. The only property reported to me for sale on any of the islands recently was on it. This was a house described only as having nine bedrooms and with one and a half acres on the shore. It was listed at fifteen thousand dollars.

## Massachusetts

According to Edward Rowe Snow, author of *The Romance of Boston Bay,* there are 150 islands along the Massachusetts coast, and 110 of them are more or less habitable. A number of these latter, however, are located in urbanized Boston Bay and are used for such unattractive purposes as a House of Correction and a plant for making fertilizer from horse carcasses. Several of the War Assets Administration's surplus islands were in Boston Bay, too, and like the W.A.A. islands in Casco Bay they were inappropriate for island retreats.

A few islands farther out in Boston Bay and on up and down the Massachusetts coast are owned by Boston businessmen who commute to and from them either daily or for week ends. Consequently, the prices usually are high. North of Boston I could find only one of the larger type of island with many summer cottages, some of which might be reasonably priced. This was Plum Island, about eight miles long, quite narrow and connected by a causeway to Newburyport. Off Marblehead, a six-acre plot on a small island was offered not long ago. It had three cottages, a seaplane hangar, a well and ship-to-shore telephone, no gas or electricity. It was listed at $12,500.

Between Boston and Cape Cod to the south there are only a few scattered small islands. One of these is the Glades, a misnamed rocky spit of land off Cohasset without a single shrub or tree but with a rambling old house. Once a summer hotel with a highly spiced reputation for the amusements it offered, it was bought some years ago by a group of old Boston families, including the Charles Francis Adamses. They made it over into apartments, each family having its own suite and servants.

South of Cape Cod in coves and lagoons along its shore and in Nantucket Sound, Vineyard Sound and Buzzards Bay are dozens of islands, ranging from Martha's Vineyard and Nantucket, both many square miles in area, down to tiny split-acre dots on the map. Martha's Vineyard and Nantucket offer a sort of compromise type of island life. Both are so big that many of the homes on them are far out of sight and sound of the sea, and both have good-sized towns with all the trappings of mainland civilization. Yet both are well out to sea (the Vineyard five miles from the nearest coast point and Nantucket over twenty miles), and you can find homes on remote coves and points where you can live much as you would on a small island. If you want to experiment with island life for a summer or two, you can rent rooms for a few dollars a week or take a whole mansion for a couple of thousand dollars or more for the season.

There are a few small islands off the shores of both the Vineyard and Nantucket, but most of the owners seem extremely reluctant to talk about them.

"One of the island's main charms for us," one wrote me, "is the fact that there are few intruders and we are able to lead the kind of life we prefer. With that in mind we are very much against any publicity, and I hope you will understand our point of view."

Extending southwest in a more or less straight line from Woods Hole on the southern tip of Cape Cod are the Elizabeth Islands, all privately owned. Naushon, the largest, about six miles long and a mile and a half wide, has been the property of the Forbes family of Boston for three generations and has scattered over it ten flamboyantly Victorian houses for various branches of the family. The current patriarch absolutely forbids automobiles and liquor. Heavily wooded, the island has a large deer population and hundreds of sheep. In some circles it is considered a great honor to be invited to the island's annual "sheeping," when everyone mounts horses, helps drive the sheep into a corral, then joins in shearing them.

Life on Cuttyhunk, another of the Elizabeths, is less strenuous. There's a small village of the same name as the island where, as one inhabitant puts it, "we have a firehouse but but haven't gotten around to a fire engine yet." The village has a couple of boardinghouses and is the only one of the Elizabeths with such accommodations for transients. Most of the island is occupied by summer homes whose owners consider the twice-a-week mailboat service from New Bedford quite sufficient contact with the outside world.

No property on these or the other Elizabeth Islands has been reported to me as currently for sale. But there are a number of tiny islands along the western and southern shore of Cape Cod which occasionally become available. The best way to investigate them would be by driving south from Buzzards Bay on Massachusetts Highway #28 to Woods Hole, then northeast along the same highway to Chatham, stopping to inquire of local real-estate dealers along the way.

## Rhode Island

In spite of the promise of its name, the State of Rhode Island and Providence Plantations (as it calls itself in full) offers very little in the way of private islands. Big Rhode Island itself, where once fabulously fashionable Newport is located, has been largely urbanized. Most of the dozen or so other islands in Narragansett Bay are Army or Navy property. A large part of one has been made into a laboratory for study of hoof-and-mouth disease in cattle by the Department of Agriculture. And the three properties offered for sale by the W.A.A. were of little interest to would-be escapees.

Block Island, eight miles out in the open Atlantic, is a popular summer resort. It can be reached by summer ferry from New London, Providence, Newport or Point Judith. There often are a few properties for sale, dozens of cottages for rent every summer, and some thirty resort hotels. It's a fine place if what you want are cool ocean breezes, good swimming and sailing, golf, tennis and such. But you will share them with hundreds of others.

## Sources of Additional Information

MAINE

*General*

Maine Development Commission
State House
Augusta, Maine
(Has several publications which it will send you on request. Among the most useful: "Hotels, Camps & Tourist Homes in Maine," "State Highway Map," "Public Parks in Maine," "Fishing," "Hunting," "Maine Salt Water Sport Fishing.")

State of Maine Publicity Bureau
Gateway Circle
Portland 4, Maine

Camden-Rockport Chamber of Commerce
Camden, Maine

*Real-Estate Dealers*

Henry M. Baribeau
52 Pleasant Street
Brunswick, Maine

Allen Insurance Agency
The Robert Block
Camden, Maine

James W. Lyons
Damariscotta, Maine

Franklin H. Wood
Court House
Rockland, Maine

Stephen A. Lavender
151 Main Street
Thomaston, Maine

A. D. Gray, Realtor
The Maine-Way
Waldoboro, Maine

## NEW HAMPSHIRE — ISLES OF SHOALS

*General*

Miss Helen L. Kelly
Chamber of Commerce
Portsmouth, New Hampshire

*Real-Estate Dealer* (for property on the Isles of Shoals):

Miss Rosamond Thaxter
Kittery Point, Maine

MASSACHUSETTS
*Real-Estate Dealers*
General:
A. Pelham Stevens
Previews, Inc.
20 Kilby Street
Boston 9, Massachusetts

Benjamin C. Tower, Realtor
35 Congress Street
Boston, Massachusetts

Nantucket:
Congdon & Coleman
50 Main Street
Nantucket, Massachusetts

Elias J. Lyon & Company
Easy Street
Nantucket, Massachusetts

Albert J. Pitkin
South Water Street
Nantucket, Massachusetts

Miss Gladys Wood
India Street
Nantucket, Massachusetts

Miss Anna E. C. Barrett
Siasconset, Massachusetts

Miss Mildred Burgess
Siasconset, Massachusetts

Albert F. Egan
Siasconset, Massachusetts

Martha's Vineyard:
Mr. and Mrs. Edward L. Stevenson
Box 501
Edgartown, Massachusetts

Mrs. Theodore L. Howell
Gay Head, Massachusetts

Mr. Henry Cronig
Vineyard Haven, Massachusetts

Miss Elizabeth H. Fenner
West Tisbury, Massachusetts

## RHODE ISLAND — BLOCK ISLAND

Block Island Chamber of Commerce
Block Island, Rhode Island

Miss Margaret Ritzinger
Vaill Hotel and Cottages
Block Island, Rhode Island

CHAPTER V

# Lake Islands of New England

W HAT," a friend of mine who owns an island off the coast of Maine asked me, "is the sense of an island on a lake? You might as well live on the mainland if you're going to be that close to it. Oh, I suppose there might be a few interesting islands out in the middle of Lake Michigan, say. But an island on any lake much smaller than the Great Lakes — where's the fun? It would be too tame."

"Tell him," replied a friend of mine who owns an island on a lake in Maine, when I quoted this outburst, "that he doesn't know what he's talking about. I like an island because it gives me privacy by surrounding me with water. I think that's why most people want islands. And a lake island has to be surrounded with water as much as a sea island, doesn't it? What's more, I'll bet we don't have half the trouble getting to and from ours that he has with his."

Your choice between the two types of islands obviously is an indisputable matter of taste. If you want sea breezes with a salty tang and if you think it's tame sailing without tides and currents to combat, you probably wouldn't be happy on a lake island. But it is true that transportation to and from a lake island usually is far simpler. The same is true of the drinking water problem. If the lake water itself isn't drinkable (and it often is), you can almost always bring in a good dependable well easily and cheaply.

You also have a far wider selection to choose from among lake islands. Though there are thousands of coastal islands for sale or rent, the available islands in the lakes of the United States and Canada number hundreds of thousands. In the lakes of New England there are at least as many islands as along the section's coast.

## Maine

According to state officials there are 2465 lakes and ponds in Maine. Some, such as Sebago Lake and Moosehead Lake, have dozens of islands. Many have none. As usual, no one ever has attempted to count the total, but the average is probably at least one per lake.

Many of the lakes in the northern part of the state are far beyond the reach of highways and railroads. Islands in a few of these are owned by sportsmen who have built camps or lodges on them. They fly up from Portland and Boston, even from as far away as New York and Philadelphia during the various hunting and fishing seasons. You can also reach many of these lake islands by canoe, and any so remote as to be reachable only in this way are likely to be quite cheap. The Maine Development Commission publishes a canoeing guide if you are interested.

But there are other islanded lakes even in the northernmost end of the state which are reachable by train and car. Eagle Lake and Portage Lake on Maine Highway #11, for instance, have islands of the hunting camp type. In Long Lake near the state's northern tip there is an island being farmed, proof that such islands are tamable.

One offered for sale was in the northern waters of Moose-head Lake, the state's largest. The property consisted of two small connecting islands and had a lodge with three bedrooms, bath, living room, dining room and kitchen, offered fully furnished. There was also a small cabin, a Delco lighting system and a protected cove for landing. But Moosehead is quite easy to reach, and the asking price was a stiff twelve thousand dollars.

If you want a trial of life on a wilderness lake island, there are several island camps on Moosehead to choose among. Big attractions, of course, are the deer and bear hunting seasons and the landlocked salmon, bass and trout fishing.

Still farther south there was a two-and-a-half-acre lake island offered with all the trappings of the easy life. It had a modernized five-bedroom house plus boathouse and bathhouse. Furnishings included a Deepfreeze, a piano, linens and silver, and an outboard motorboat and a rowboat were thrown in. The asking price: fifteen thousand dollars.

But it is also possible to find islands without such comparatively expensive homes. One is in Lake Megunticook, just three miles inland from the coast at Camden. Half an acre in size, it has a white sand beach, pine woods and a fine view of surrounding hills. Right-of-way privileges on the mainland go with it. Without buildings of any kind, the asking price was $2750.

Back inland again, there is a whole constellation of lakes with islands in the Augusta area. The Belgrade Lakes, the Kennebec Lakes and China Lake with its satellite ponds all have islands both large and small. It is an island on Lake Maranacook in this region that the New York City school-teaching couple I mentioned in Chapter I have made a summer paradise. They bought the one-acre island some twenty years ago complete with a five-bedroom bungalow, a sleeping porch and a separate studio building for only thirty-five hundred dollars. Prices, of course, have gone up considerably since then. But islands are so numerous in the area that if you can take time to look around at length, you have a good chance of finding something similar to this even today in the lower part of the five- to ten-thousand-dollar range.

There are several other groups of heavily islanded lakes, such as the Graham Lake region east of Bangor and the Rangeley Lakes in the northwest corner of the state. But one of the most appealing is the Sebago group — Sebago Lake, Little Sebago Lake, Long Lake, Panther Pond and several others. Nearly all are within less than an hour's drive north of Portland. Sebago Lake alone has dozens of islands, and most of the others have at least a few.

One of the most enthusiastic islanders I ever met is a young Boston photographer, John Stuart Cloud, who bought a Sebago Lake island in 1948. Fortunately, John and his wife Barbara contracted their virulent cases of island fever at the same time. It began with visions of an idyllic week-end and vacation life on a green and pleasant islet within a couple of hours' driving time from their Boston home.

"Also," as John told me the story, "we have a monkey, and Josephine is somewhat antisocial so far as women are concerned and somewhat of a problem so far as we are concerned. We thought that on a small island, say about two hundred feet in diameter, we could turn Josephine loose and still keep an eye on her.

"We hired a plane and instructed the pilot to fly us around the Sebago Lakes so we could look at islands. Well, from the air a two-hundred-foot island looks awfully small, and the longer we flew and the more we looked, the more we convinced ourselves that we could use a larger island. Finally, we picked out one that seemed to have everything we wanted —

lots of trees and rocks and a natural cove on the sheltered side and plenty of space. We landed at South Casco to inquire about the owner, found him first off and made a deal without any trouble at all." (Although John never has been specific, I understand that the price was in the neighborhood of a thousand dollars.)

"Our island is Inner Green, one of a group of six — the Dingley Islands — in the northeast corner of Sebago Lake. It's about eight acres in size, a quarter mile offshore, twenty-five miles from Portland and about a three-hour drive from Boston. And, of course, the first thing we discovered the first time we visited it was that Josephine could swim. So we still have to keep her tied, but we can at least tie her in a different place every day and give her a little variety."

Some of the Clouds' experiences in fitting out their island are the sort of thing from which other would-be islanders can learn if they feel inclined to take lessons. John naturally first set about looking for a boat. He decided that he wanted a small one with an outboard motor but that it had to be rugged enough to haul lumber and supplies for building. The only ones he could find near Lake Sebago were too flimsy, but he found just what he wanted in Boston. That, however, left him with the problem of getting it to the lake. In an intrepid moment he rented a cradle trailer, loaded the boat on it and hooked it to his car. Then he began to be dubious about his own lack of experience in trailer hauling and about the obvious bad fit of the boat on the trailer. His fears proved quite justified in the second case. Every time he came to a stop light on the trip, the boat slipped and had to be refastened in place. And by the time he reached South Casco, there were deep gouges in both sides of the boat. It took fairly expensive repair and repainting jobs to make it lakeworthy.

Next came the problem of a temporary shelter for the first

couple of years while they cut out dead trees, cleared rocks from a beach and built a permanent house. They solved this more or less satisfactorily by pitching a 16′ × 16′ surplus Army tent.

"But," as John told me the story, "at that point something went wrong with my thinking and I insisted that what we needed was an all-metal prefabricated hut. I knew of one which was being used on a parking lot in Boston and which I could get for nothing. All I had to do was take it apart and truck it to Maine — simple as that. So I started taking it apart — and found that all the bolt threads were rusted solid and that someone had poured four inches of concrete in and around the hut after it had been set up. I talked to myself about pioneer stuff, got a chisel and sledge hammer, cut bolts and cracked cement until I was about dead, then discovered that the ends of the hut were all one piece, couldn't conceivably be taken apart and were much too large to put in the boat if and when I ever did get them to Maine.

"By that time I was mad. I hired a truck, shipped the stuff to the lake, borrowed two boats, tied the metal hut parts across them and towed them to Inner Green. Week-end guests helped lug them to the site we picked. Then, of course, I had forgotten which pieces went where. Also, in my enthusiasm with the sledge, I had just about ruined the bottoms of the panels. So the only thing to do was finish with vertical wooden siding over the metal framework. But you can't nail wood to metal, and we had to make a frame of two-by-fours. By the time we finished, the roof kind of sagged and the walls leaned a little to windward, but we were able at least to store our tent and stuff in it for that winter."

In spite of these troubles the Clouds made up their minds that there were to be "no carpenters allowed" on the island and that they would do all the building themselves, with the help of guests. But when I told part of their story in the *Saturday Evening Post* article which launched me on my hunt for islands, several students at a Boston building trades school read it and offered to lend a hand in return for a couple of weeks' vacation on Inner Green. They helped start the Clouds on a neat little cottage with a nonsagging roof and nonleaning walls.

All in all, the island is now one of the tidiest little private kingdoms you will find anywhere. The Clouds cook on gasoline stoves, use gasoline lamps for light and get excellent drinking and washing water from the lake (it is the city of Portland's source of water, too, and regulations keep it permanently pure). Wild rice, musk grass and coontail which they planted in one cove attract hordes of ducks every fall, and there usually are partridge around and plenty of fish just offshore. A small cabin houses guests and frees Barbara from all concern with making their beds and such (she leaves it to them). And to cap it all the Clouds have been able to buy a small Piper seaplane, have learned to fly it and now can commute from Boston to the island daily when they feel like it.

The plane has proved a fine investment in other ways, too. Through it the Clouds have met a number of seaplane fliers in the area. They drop in at the island frequently for coffee. Now and then a group assembles there and flies off to the northern lakes for fishing.

On these trips the Clouds have worked out an ingenious camping arrangement. When they find a good fishing spot, they anchor the plane and tie hammocks to the tie-down rings under the wings. This provides perfect shelter in case of rain.

"Also," says John, "it's really living to throw out an anchor and let the plane weathercock with the wind and rock us to sleep. It sounds like playboy stuff, and I certainly would have thought it was before we tried it. But actually it's less expensive to make these trips by plane than it is to drive. We burn about four and a half gallons of gas per hour and can cover an average of a hundred and ten miles an hour. And it's fewer miles by air."

Familiarity with the plane has made the Clouds remarkably casual about it. For instance, when Barbara runs out of sugar, butter or such, there are no neighbors to whom she can apply for a loan. So she climbs into the plane and hops down to the grocery store at Naples, seven miles away.

Not far from the Clouds' island is one owned by Mrs. Richie C. Magee of Altamont, New York. Mrs. Magee and her sister, who shares the island with her, like to describe themselves quite inaccurately as "two rather Grant-Woodish old ladies." Their lively enjoyment of their island mocks the phrase.

They bought it in 1946 unencumbered with any buildings. Named Outer Spectacle, it is about the two hundred feet in diameter which the Clouds originally had in mind, heavily wooded with oak, maple, birch, pine and fir, and with wild roses growing everywhere. In 1946 they were unable to get the lumber to start building, and in 1947 they couldn't find carpenters. But they persisted, and by the end of 1948 they had exactly what they wanted — a bright, cheerful, three-bedroom house with pine paneling throughout and plenty of room for guests.

"And," says Mrs. Magee, "Maine workmen are wonderful. Every single price they charged us for the building work was under the minimum estimate they had made us in advance. They were so nice to us that we wanted to do something to celebrate when they finished working so we bought some ale for them. They were very pleasant about it, but they said they would much rather have tea."

The way they built the dock is of interest to all north-country islanders. Instead of assembling it on the shore, then laboriously hauling it out into the water, they built it on the ice during the winter, and it sank into place in the spring thaw.

The two sisters usually go up to the island in May and stay nearly all the time until September. Mrs. Magee's first step was to learn to run the outboard motor. "It took a whole season," as she tells the story, "for me to discover that it could be put into reverse, but we got along. I knew I was going to run ashore sooner or later, and once I had done it and gotten off I wasn't a bit scared."

She admits she was scared, though, the time a bull moose swam ashore. But it swam off again without damage to anyone or anything. And she is quite proud of her story about the time she and her friends were the only ones fishing in the lake who were catching anything. Other fishermen inquired what they were using for bait and were appalled to learn that their success was due to the tactic of impaling worms on fly hooks.

Like most islanders she wants complete informality and thinks it's quite a joke when guests come laden with numerous suitcases because they imagine that a private island must be a very grand sort of place. Fishing and swimming — the water is unpredictably laced with warm and cold currents which make the latter, in her opinion, special fun — are the two chief diversions she offers guests. The other is "rock hopping," her own invention.

"I never in my life had enough moonlight before I came to the island," she told me. "So now when the moon is out, we all put on shoes with crepe rubber soles and hop from rock to rock around the island."

Neither the Clouds' nor Mrs. Magee's islands were specifically for sale when they bought them. They found the local owners, made offers and struck bargains. There are many others which can be dealt for in the same way.

## New Hampshire

According to state authorities there are more than thirteen hundred lakes and ponds in New Hampshire. They are of the same origin as those of Maine, having been scooped out by the glaciers of the ice age which deposited here and there among them big piles of sand, gravel and rocks to form islands. The total number of islands seems to be considerably smaller than in Maine, but they are so numerous that a good-sized lake without an island is a rarity. Indeed, publicists for Lake Ossipee, six miles long and three wide, consider it a claim to fame that it is the largest body of water in the state without an island.

"Its placid countenance," they put it, "is unbroken by even the tiniest islet."

A number of New Hampshire islands are scattered in more or less isolated lakes from one end of the state to the other. But the chief concentration, and what seems to be the most interesting ones, are in the lake region centering around big Lake Winnipesaukee in the east central part of the state. By a conservative estimate there must be at least five hundred islands in this area.

The biggest group is on Lake Winnipesaukee. With 283 miles of shoreline but only 72 square miles of water surface, this lake consists largely of bays, coves and backwaters with islands large and small in every part. It is another of those bodies of water which are supposed to have exactly 365 islands — "One," some local boy scout enthusiast wrote, "for each good deed done in a year." But in this case a count has been made. According to the Lakes Region Association, Winnipesaukee has 274 habitable islands, perhaps indicating that the Scouts of the area have grown a bit lax in performing their duties.

Principal approaches to the lake are through Laconia, The Weirs and Meredith to the east, Center Harbor to the north. Alton Bay to the south and Wolfeboro to the southeast. The last town claims to be the first North American summer resort, basing its claim on a big summer home built there in 1768 by the then Royal Administrator of New Hampshire. Much of the area, including many of the islands, is devoted to large and aged but well-preserved summer homes.

There are a number of large islands in the multifamily class where cottages and building acreages are available. Governor's Island, off The Weirs, has some seventy-five homes and more being built. A few usually are for rent. As on most such islands, its property owners have organized an association to finance and operate community services.

Squam Lake, a few miles northwest of Winnipesaukee, also has numerous islands. It is less accessible than the bigger lake, and the only town near its shore is Holderness. Many of the properties on and around it are in the big-estate class, but there also are a few cottages and camping islands.

## Vermont

Like Maine and New Hampshire, Vermont has numerous glacier-made lakes scattered throughout the state, and many of them have islands of assorted sizes. But the greatest number are in the northern part of the state, and the only large concentration is in Lake Champlain.

Undoubtedly the most famous of Vermont's private islands, and one of the most intriguing I have heard of anywhere, is Neshobe Island in Lake Bomoseen, a few miles west of Rutland. It was the seat and reason for existence of the Neshobe Island Club, whose members included Harpo Marx, Russel Crouse, Neysa McMein and several other refugees from the Hotel Algonquin Round Table in New York City. But it was ruled to the almost complete exclusion of any contradiction by the witty and determinedly unwise Alexander Woollcott.

In 1936 Woollcott built his own home on the island, far outshining in luxury the club's original quarters, and by the end of his life was spending six months of the year there. He summoned and dismissed both club members and other friends with regal condescension and permitted no deviation from whatever routine he decreed for the day. It was here that, according to a probably apocryphal story, in one of the diabolical moods which sometimes seized him he planted a recording machine under the bed of a female movie star whom he suspected of dalliance with a male guest, then played the resulting record at the communal breakfast.

Local fishermen who happened to pass near the island sometimes told tales of hearing bloodcurdling screams and wild, impassioned quarrels. In all likelihood they had chanced by during a croquet game. It was Woollcott's favorite sport, and he decreed a game almost every day. It began at 11 A.M., lasted at least three hours and usually aroused the participants to great outbursts of verbal violence.

After Woollcott's death the property was put up for sale or rent and still remained on the market the last I heard. The island is seven acres in area, about half a mile offshore and beautifully wooded. From the air it justifies the favorite island cliché simile "gemlike," resembling an oval emerald in a blue setting. The house Woollcott built is of fieldstone with ten rooms, and the old clubhouse is a ten-room frame building. There's also a barn with a bedroom, workshop and boat storage space. All are offered fully furnished at an asking price reported to me variously as $100,000 and $62,500.

To the north of Bomoseen in Lake Champlain you can take your pick of a considerable number of islands which range most of the way to the other end of the scale in price. There are several in the one- to ten-acre range which have been altered scarcely at all from the state in which the Indians found them and which probably can be had for a very few hundred dollars. Some, particularly the larger ones which make up Vermont's Grand Isle County, are devoted to farming or to summer tourists. Others are comparable to Neshobe in luxury.

Nine-acre Fishbladder Island, for instance, is two miles out in the lake from the town of Grand Isle. It was offered with a fourteen-room lodge, a four-room cottage, several other buildings all fully furnished, seven assorted boats ranging from a thirty-foot launch to a canoe, plus power mowers for the lawns, at an asking price of $75,000. But the asking price on one-and-a-half-acre Button Island near Vergennes, with a pleasant eleven-room house and all utilities plus a boathouse and icehouse, was $19,500.

Another farther down the lake off Long Point is Gardiner's Island. It is or was owned by Harry A. Weibel, a New York City fur dealer, covers three acres and has an eight-room house with pine paneling in several rooms. But the remarkable thing about it is that it is the only lake island I have discovered which has a buried treasure legend. The story is that after Ethan Allen's capture of nearby Fort Ticonderoga during the Revolutionary War, several British soldiers who had escaped were seen carrying a heavy box onto the island. They left without it. Naturally, there has been a great deal of digging, but as usual no one has reported having any luck.

## Massachusetts, Connecticut and Rhode Island

All three of the smaller New England states have numerous scattered small lakes. A few such lakes have islands, but there seem to be no large island concentrations. I found only one lake island property in any of the three states which was for sale recently. This was a one-acre plot on an island in Connecticut's Bantam Lake, near Litchfield, and it included a large and expensive summer home.

Massachusetts's Lake Chargoggagoggmanchaugagoggchaubunagungamaugg — a name which probably has caused more people to swallow their tongues than any other this side of Wales — has an island typical of the area. It's owned by two families who have shared it for decades as a summer home. The younger generations of the two families have intermarried "just to keep the island to themselves," as one friend of both families told me jokingly.

I turned up one case of a New England island whose owners acquired it by the nowadays unusual and always the most inexpensive method possible — by establishing squatters' rights. In 1913 a Bridgeport, Connecticut, man, Everett Cartwright (now President Emeritus of the University of Bridgeport), was looking for a place to set up a vacation camp with his family on the upper reaches of the Housatonic River near New Milford. A pleasantly wooded two-acre island just below the river's Great Falls seemed just the place. Nobody seemed to own it, and nearby farmers told him that it must belong to the state.

Professor Cartwright thought this unlikely because the river was not navigable at that point. (State or Federal officials can claim authority over islands in navigable rivers because they are responsible for keeping them navigable.) But he wrote to Connecticut's secretary of state asking permission to camp on the island and was told that if the state did own the island, which the secretary doubted, he was perfectly welcome to camp on it. The following year the professor returned to the island, built a small cabin on it and quietly began paying taxes to establish his claim. This, however, was not sufficient to establish it beyond all doubt. So he later leased one end of the island to a friend. When the lease had gone unchallenged for seventeen years, the island officially became his property by the laws of the State of Connecticut.

In all likelihood there are other such squattable islands in other rivers around the country. State laws concerning such properties vary, though, and in some places might make the owner of the nearest mainland property the owner of the island if he wanted to assert his rights. Also, there is one important drawback to most river islands. Every spring there is a chance that part of your island will become, at least temporarily, a part of the river bottom. Chiefly for that reason, Professor Cartwright's daughter is, or was, considering selling their island.

## Sources of Additional Information

MAINE

*General*

Maine Development Commission
State House
Augusta, Maine
  (Has two publications of special interest: "Hotels, Camps & Tourist Homes in Maine" and "Maine — Fishing, Hunting, Canoeing.")

Moosehead Information Center
Greenville, Maine

*Real-Estate Dealers*

Allen Insurance Agency
The Robert Block
Camden, Maine

Albert L. Kavanagh Realty Company
501 Main Street
Lewiston, Maine

Phil Marx
36 Exchange Street
Rumford, Maine

A. D. Gray, Realtor
The Maine-way
Waldoboro, Maine

## NEW HAMPSHIRE

*General*

New Hampshire State Planning and Development Commission
Concord, New Hampshire

The Lakes Region Association
South Main Street
Wolfeboro, New Hampshire

*Real-Estate Dealers*

Previews, Inc.
20 Kilby Street
Boston 9, Massachusetts

Reuben N. Hodge
Center Sandwich, New Hampshire

Lamprey & Lamprey
Weirs Boulevard
Laconia, New Hampshire

Lloyd D. Lund
104 Pleasant Street
Meredith, New Hampshire

Clarence M. Mixer & Son
8 North Main Street
Wolfeboro, New Hampshire

## VERMONT

*General*
Publicity Service
State Development Commission
Montpelier, Vermont

*Real-Estate Dealers*
C. Russell Little
Fair Haven, Vermont

M. E. Walbridge Agency, Inc.
41½ Merchants Row
Rutland, Vermont

CHAPTER VI

# The Thousand Islands and Others in New York State and Southeastern Ontario

NEW YORK STATE shares the Thousand Islands with the Province of Ontario, and there are others in south-eastern Ontario which have more in common with these than with the islands farther west in the province. In addition, hundreds of others are scattered throughout the lakes and rivers of the interior of New York. I have brought them all together in this chapter because they share more with each other than with those of any of the surrounding areas.

## *The Thousand Islands*

In early June two years ago two friends of mine, a couple who live in New York City, set off by car on a vacation trip. They planned a leisurely drive via Montreal and Quebec out to the Gaspé Peninsula. But having listened patiently for many months to my talk of islands, they decided to make a short detour and cross into Canada via the Thousand Islands Bridge in order to see the islands. They never got any farther.

After spending a night in a tourist cabin near Alexandria Bay, New York, they intended to drive slowly across the bridge (it consists of five spans which hop from island to island, covering seven miles altogether from mainland to mainland) and to confine their island sight-seeing to gawking from the bridge. But at breakfast in the village they saw an advertisement for a "fifty-mile ramble," a three-hour motorboat tour among the islands. It was a beautiful day, and the idea intrigued them. They set off on the boat's first trip of the day.

The first part of the trip wound past a "millionaires' row" group of islands, including Heart Island and its Boldt Castle which I mentioned in the first chapter. Most of them had huge and obviously expensive homes. Farther out they passed dozens of others with more privacy and far less expensive looks. Without any really serious interest they asked the guide whether any of these were ever rented. He pointed out several which were unoccupied and available and referred them to a real-estate dealer.

By the time they got back to Alexandria Bay they had begun speculating about whether they really wanted to spend their vacation driving from one place to another. They looked up the real-estate man their guide had mentioned. Before they quite realized what had happened, he had bundled them into another motorboat and was giving them their choice of seven cottages, each with an island all to itself, at prices ranging from five hundred to a thousand dollars for the season. Every summer since, they have returned to the one they rented.

"We never really knew," they have told me, "what a vacation meant before. Once a day a water taxi brings us our mail and groceries. The rest of the time we have our whole world to ourselves."

The availability of all this in the Thousand Islands to families with modest vacation budgets is a comparatively recent development. The area was launched as a summer resort for the wealthy more than a hundred years ago, and until 1929 and the Crash it remained chiefly that. Since then the big money has not been able to afford keeping the islands to itself. Because they are easy to reach in a day's driving from most of the country east of Detroit and north of Washington — 345 miles from New York City or Philadelphia, 365 from Boston, 475 from Washington and 500 from Detroit — their popularity has steadily increased, though they are still far from cheap.

Stretching for some forty miles downstream from the point where Lake Ontario narrows into the St. Lawrence River, they are among the very few groups of islands which have been counted. The trouble is, they have been counted too often and by too many different people. Various authorities have told me that they number 1690, 1792 and over 1800. They have also told me variously (1) that the international boundary divides the group approximately half and half between the United States and Canada, and (2) that it puts two thirds of the islands in Canada. One reason for all this variance is that the water level rises and falls slightly from year to year and sometimes covers those islands which lie very low. In any case it is certain that "Thousand Islands" is a considerable understatement.

Nearly all are privately owned. On parts of four large islands and all of smaller Cedar Island, New York maintains state parks which have excellent camping facilities. There are several resort hotels and cottage groups on other islands, and a few of the larger ones such as Grindstone Island and

Wolfe Island are devoted mostly to farming. But the great majority are the kind of retreats designed for escape from civilization which the word "island" calls up in the minds of most people.

Among this majority there still remain dozens which have not been built upon and which can be had for as little as five hundred dollars. In fact, one little quarter-acre bit of rock-bound greenery was offered to me for fifty dollars. But for anything of two or three acres with a good landing you probably would find the price tag reading at least in four figures. And an island with a livable home and utilities and a price in the neighborhood of five thousand dollars probably would be a rare bargain. The chief attraction of the region to those who want to keep expenses to a minimum is that many of the islands can be rented for a season at quite reasonable prices.

If you want to explore the islands, one of the numerous motorboat cruises is a good way to start. Or you can be even more thorough and start with a look around via one of the many planes for hire. Chief jumping-off points are Alexandria Bay, Clayton and Cape Vincent on the New York side and Gananoque and Kingston on the Ontario side.

You could, of course, take your own boat or hire one, but if you do, be sure to equip yourself with good charts and a knowledge of how to read them. The islands form a maze in which it is very easy to get lost. In fact, the maze is so complex that one of the last of the old-time pirates held out in it for a year against the combined forces of the United States and Canada. He was Wild Bill Johnston, who called himself the Admiral of the Thousand Islands. In 1837 several over-enthusiastic United States citizens decided to "free" Canada from British rule and launched the brief Patriots' War. It fizzled quickly when the Canadians resisted their liberation, but it gave Johnston, one of its participants, a taste for adventure. He organized an independent navy of twenty-two men and three rowboats, raided in and out of the islands, sank a British ship and in general had a fine time until he was caught. Apparently no one held his fling against him because instead of being hanged he wound up as a lighthouse keeper on one of the islands.

Wood-burning steamers of Johnston's day used to put in at the islands for fuel and almost completely denuded most of them. But new growth has re-covered them, and they have magnificent stands of both hardwoods and evergreens. Many of the larger ones also have plentiful game and, of course, good fishing in the surrounding waters.

One of the most enthusiastic of the island owners in the area is Edward J. Noble, chairman of the board of the Life Savers Corporation and of the American Broadcasting Company. Born and raised in Gouverneur, New York, thirty miles inland from the islands, he was fascinated by them and dreamed of owning one. In his childhood, though, such an ambition seemed attainable only if you didn't have to ask the price. The islands were then the playthings of the Pullmans of the Pullman Car Company, the Wheelers of Standard Oil, and other families possessed of similar fortunes.

When Noble's candy-with-the-hole-in-the-middle caught the public's fancy in the early twenties, he suddenly found himself in that financially lofty company. One of his first indulgences was buying half a dozen of the Thousand Islands owned by the George Boldt estate. These included four small islands and a huge section of big Wellesley Island, equipped with a polo field and a golf course, which Noble turned into a country club.

Also included was Heart Island and its Boldt Castle, a white elephant with a high tax which he didn't want but which the estate trustees firmly insisted he must take along with the rest. Noble paid the taxes, installed a caretaker on the island and forgot about it, with amusing results. For the white elephant was put to work. Several years later the caretaker died, leaving his heirs a small fortune consisting chiefly of his savings from the tips given him by tourists whom he had taken on tours of the castle. Now there is a regular charge for the tour, and the proceeds, averaging fifty thousand dollars a year, go to a charitable foundation established by Noble.

Typical of most modern island owners, including those in the top financial brackets, and quite unlike the old-timers, Noble has not gone in for any attention-getting mansion building. The island he prefers is remote Journey's End, far over on the Canadian side. Only five acres in area, it has a comparatively simple ten-room house where he vacations during the summer. In the spring and fall he occasionally stays at a log cabin on his Wellesley Island property. In winter he goes to an island he owns off the South Carolina coast, of which more later.

"I guess," he told me, "you might say that I am addicted to islands."

## Southeastern Ontario

Southeastern Ontario stretches from the northeast shore of Lake Ontario eastward along the St. Lawrence River and north to the Quebec border. It is one of the most heavily populated parts of the province. Even so, it includes many spaces which are fairly wide open, and it is easily accessible from all parts of the northeastern United States. It has dozens of lakes with islands, three hundred in one lake alone. Unfortunately, few, if any, are Crown lands available under the terms described in Chapter III. Like the Canadian portion of the Thousand Islands, most have been bought up by private individuals in the last few decades, but they often can be rented and occasionally come up for sale.

Along the northeastern shore of Lake Ontario are a couple of dozen islands, including big and populous "Quinte's Isle of Lakes and Bays." Among the most interesting is Main Duck Island, twenty-five miles out in Lake Ontario. Like most of those in this area, it was purchased from the Crown about thirty years ago by a local man. Thirteen years ago he sold it to John Foster Dulles, now Secretary of State.

Dulles and his wife go to the island for a week or two several times during the year from early spring to late fall. It covers a thousand acres and extends for two and a half miles. Because it is near the approach to the St. Lawrence entrance and has a dangerous shoal along one side, it used to be the scene of many wrecks, and odd flotsam and jetsam still can be found around its shores. Now the Canadian government maintains a lighthouse at one end, and at a small cove on the north shore there are a dozen shacks occasionally used by commercial fishermen working the area.

But the Dulleses have the rest of it completely to themselves. They live in a small log cabin which they had built from cedar trees in the old Indian fashion by a group of Indians they brought down from northern Ontario for the purpose. They take no servants to the island, preferring to do all their own work while there. Occasionally they are completely cut off from the outside by stormy weather, but they usually get supplies and mail daily by plane from Watertown, New York.

Some years ago there were buffalo roaming the island, but they failed to reproduce and died off. Around fifty deer still live on it, though, and Dulles shoots a few every fall to keep the number low enough for the amount of winter forage available to them. Now and then a young buck will try to swim to the mainland, but none ever has been known to accomplish the twenty-five-mile swim.

"The island," Dulles told me, "seems to be on the main passage for migratory birds. I try to go up every spring as soon as the ice goes out to watch the birds come through. During one April week I counted seventy-five varieties. And there is a pair of bald-headed eagles which have nested for many years on nearby Yorkshire Island."

Like most of Canada, this area is seeking to attract American visitors, and if you want to explore for islands, you will get plenty of help and suggestions in Picton on the Isle of Quinte about those which might be for sale or rent. The Isle of Quinte itself has lakes containing islands, if you want something as complicated as an island on a lake in an island on a lake. It also has the mysterious and picturesque Lake-on-the-Mountain, a small lake at the top of a hill which towers almost perpendicularly two hundred feet above the Bay of Quinte. What makes it mysterious is that there is no visible inlet or outlet for its clear, cold water and no apparent reason for its existence.

But you will find a wider choice of islands on the Rideau Lakes Waterway, a chain of lakes connected by canals and locks which extends from Kingston, Ontario, northeastward to Ottawa, much like the Trent Canal route which runs from a point farther west on Lake Ontario to Georgian Bay on Lake Huron. It makes a fine, quiet cruise, or you can do it in a canoe since there are no currents to battle. There are plenty of places to camp out along the way, and there also are hotels and cabins if you want more comfort.

You will find islands all along the route. Nearly all the lakes have at least a few. Cranberry Lake and Newboro Lake near the southern end have scores. Big Rideau Lake at the midway point has at least three hundred, and it is likely that you would be able to find a considerable choice available with livable cottages or cabins at well under five thousand dollars. And in the dozens of less accessible lakes scattered to the west of the route you will find an even wider choice at still lower prices.

## New York State

Although northwestern New York State has some of the world's most beautiful lakes, they are almost completely devoid of islands. It is a pity, because an island in Cayuga Lake or Keuka Lake or any of the other Finger Lakes with their steep surrounding cliffs would make a wonderful place to live. The only island in any of them is Squaw Island in Canandaigua Lake, and it is a State Museum Reservation devoted to the oddest exhibits I ever heard of. These are "water biscuits" built up by alternate layers of lime and fossilized algae deposited on pebbles. It seems that it was by studying the process of formation of these "water biscuits" on Squaw Island that geologists first learned how ocean reefs of a certain type are formed.

The northeastern part of the state, on the other hand, has several hundred lakes with at least several hundred and possibly a couple of thousand islands, plus a good many in rivers. A number of the latter are scattered in the St. Lawrence downstream from the Thousand Island area. Most of these are near Waddington in the International Rapids section of the river. Wild and undeveloped, they are used for little except fishing and duck hunting. Even so, they would not come cheap. If the legislation needed to launch the St. Lawrence seaway and power development project ever escapes from the morass of Congressional lobbying in which it has been bogged for several years, the area probably will become a huge industrial center.

South of the St. Lawrence lie the Adirondacks, where lakes are scattered thickly. Many have islands used chiefly for summer homes and hunting lodges. There are a few along the New York side of Lake Champlain, but the most interesting and most numerous group are the Lake George islands. They number either 155 or 167, depending on which state authority does the counting. By 1876 about thirty of them had been sold or granted to private citizens by the state. In that year the state legislature passed a bill preventing further sales and making the islands a part of the forest preserve. Later, the State Conservation Department began issuing permits to campers who wanted to vacation on the islands. Every summer now hundreds of vacationers enjoy an island idyl for periods ranging from a week end to several weeks, and it's all free.

Altogether there are about five hundred camp sites on the 120 state-owned islands, so you don't have an island all to yourself. Many of the smaller ones, however, have only two or three camps, and all are so arranged that they are well out of sight of each other. But you do have to obey certain rules. If you plan to stay more than three days, you must get a camping permit from the Forest Ranger on Glen Island near Bolton Landing. It's good for two weeks and can be renewed for successive two-week periods, the total time permissible depending on the season, the individual island you choose and the number of others seeking camp sites. Usually, it is possible to stay at least six weeks if you wish, and some have stretched their stay through the whole summer.

Sanitary regulations are rigidly enforced, and they have been so successful that the lake water remains quite drinkable. Because sound carries so far and so distinctly over water, you have to be reasonably quiet between 10 P.M. and 7 A.M.

And for some unexplained reason, if you take along your dog or even your cat, you are supposed to keep it on a leash at all times.

Most of the camp sites consist of a small beach and landing place, a wooden tent platform and a fireplace. You supply the rest of your equipment, and many of the regulars store theirs on the mainland between summers. There are several outfitters at Bolton Landing and other villages on the lake who specialize in renting equipment to island campers. At a rate of twenty-five or thirty dollars a week for two persons, depending on the season, one of these provides you with an eighteen-foot canoe and paddles, a tent, folding cots, a kerosene lantern, cooking utensils, dishes, silverware and sundry odds and ends (an outboard motor for the canoe costs ten dollars a week extra). You have to provide only blankets (you will want at least three apiece), linens, clothes and food.

All of which may sound either too strenuous or too public for many island dreamers. But there are a number of families who have been camping on Lake George islands every summer for two generations. The wooded hills towering along both sides of the lake, the cool clarity of the air and the water, the calls of whippoorwills echoing in the evening, the camaraderie of visiting back and forth with other islanders — "It wouldn't be a summer without all that," one old-timer told me.

You can have all that without camping out, however. On some of the privately owned Lake George islands there are lodges which take in summer boarders. And every summer there are a few cottages and houses for rent on others, mostly by the season. Most of the state-owned islands are concentrated near the center of the lake in the region called The Narrows, and the private ones are scattered to the north and south so that most of them are fairly isolated.

South of Lake George the lakes thin out, and you have to hunt carefully to find islands. There are a few scattered along the Hudson River, mostly between Glens Falls and Pough- keepsie, which are worth a look. One near Saratoga Springs was advertised for sale some time ago. It covered two and a half acres, had a five-room cottage and a garage on the main- land, and was quoted at $3750.

One of the best-known Hudson River islands, to many people a dark mystery, is Bannerman's Island just south of Beacon. Its turreted "castle" has drawn the eyes of thousands of passengers on trains which pass along the shore nearby, and yachtsmen cruising along the river have told lurid tales of being ordered away from its shores at the point of a gun. But the facts about it are comparatively dull. The castle is only a twelve-room house built some fifty years ago, in the ginger- bread style then current, by Francis Bannerman, a New York City dealer in guns and ammunition. His sons have continued in the business and now use the island chiefly for storing their stock in trade. Guards set over such a storehouse are naturally a bit inhospitable.

Still farther south in the New York City commuting area there are a few small lakes with islands. A couple of years ago two in Lake Mahopac, just over the Westchester border in Putnam County, were auctioned off.

One was forty-four-acre Canopus Island. It included a ten-room main house for which luxurious is the only word, a guest cottage, a boathouse and a view from a point 111 feet above the lake surface, plus a garage and four-room apart- ment on the mainland within four blocks of the railroad sta- tion. It was knocked down for $29,000. The other was Petra Island, thirteen acres with only the shell of a small cottage. It went for $10,300.

Altogether there are at least thirty or forty such privately owned lake islands in New York, New Jersey and Connecticut within commuting range of Manhattan. There are many others along the coast, particularly in Long Island Sound. But they belong in the next chapter.

## Sources of Additional Information

NEW YORK STATE — GENERAL

Travel Bureau
Department of Commerce
112 State Street
Albany 7, New York

SOUTHEASTERN ONTARIO — GENERAL

Division of Land and Recreational Areas
Department of Lands and Forests
Parliament Buildings
Toronto, Ontario, Canada

Department of Travel and Publicity
Parliament Buildings
Toronto, Ontario, Canada

THE THOUSAND ISLANDS
*General*

Chamber of Commerce
Alexandria Bay, New York

Thousand Islands Bridge Authority
Collins Landing
Alexandria Bay, New York

Chamber of Commerce
Clayton, New York

Jefferson County Publicity Committee
County Building
Watertown, New York

*Real-Estate Dealers*
  Charles M. Becker
  2 Church Street
  Alexandria Bay, New York

  Wiltse & DeYoung
  Bank Building
  Alexandria Bay, New York

  Thousand Islands Realty Company
  Streets Agency
  Clayton, New York

  Previews, Inc.
  49 East 53rd Street
  New York 22, N. Y.

## GENERAL INFORMATION — SPECIFIC AREAS

  Rideau Lakes Route:
  Rideau District Forester
  Department of Lands and Forests
  Kemptville, Ontario, Canada

  Canadian Hydrographic Service
  Department of Mines and Resources
  Ottawa, Ontario, Canada
    (For charts.)

  Lake Champlain:
  Chamber of Commerce
  Plattsburgh, New York

  Lake George:
  Port Jerry Estates
  Bolton Landing, New York

  Warren County Publicity Committee
  County Building
  Lake George, New York

  Chamber of Commerce
  Ticonderoga, New York

CHAPTER VII

# Coastal Islands from Connecticut to Virginia

IN ALL THE NATION's forty-five thousand miles of salt-water coastline, there are less than ten thousand miles of easily accessible, broad, sandy beach. The rest of the coast is edged by more or less steep and rocky cliffs. The greatest stretches of welcoming beach are along the Atlantic Coast from Cape Cod south. Along most of this area the land slopes gently down to the sea, and the sea floor continues this slow descent far to the east, creating a wide, shallow continental shelf.

But it is an insistent slope eastward, and few islands rise up from it very far offshore. Salt marshes and lagoons punctuate the coastline at frequent intervals, though, and give haven to hundreds of sand islands. Without such haven the surf in most cases would pull the islands back under water sooner or later. There are also in the area to be covered in this chapter two big semienclosures — Long Island Sound and Chesapeake Bay — whose outer barriers have borne most of the brunt of the surf and permitted the formation of large numbers of islands along their inner shores. Some of the Long Island area islands are of glacial origin and have rocky anchors, but on the seaward side where the surf pounds away unabated there is a constant crumbling away of the sandy shores of the islands.

Altogether, there are at least a thousand more or less habitable salt-water islands in the stretch of coast between the eastern border of Connecticut and the southern border of Virginia. Except for a few set aside for public recreation by states and municipalities they are privately owned. Some are outside the scope of this book since it is intended as a guide for those who want to escape from, and not to, such concrete and asphalt wildernesses as Manhattan Island.

## *Connecticut*

According to an official of the Connecticut State Board of Fisheries & Game who regularly patrols the coast, there are "probably about eighty" habitable islands along the Connecticut shore. They are scattered from one end to the other of its hundred-mile, crow-flight length. Most are isolated or in groups of two or three, and only a few acres in size. Nearly all the desirable ones have homes or cottages.

The only big group is the Thimble Islands, twenty being inhabited out of a total of thirty. They lie about a mile off Stony Creek, a few miles east of New Haven. Most populous of the group is Money Island, with twenty-nine homes ranging from prefabricated semicabins to large cottages. Several of the smaller ones are owned by single families who have built imposing mansions on them.

Mrs. Gertrude Gray Single of West Hartford is an unofficial but devoted chronicler of the Thimbles. She and Arthur

Single, her husband, have a summer home on Governors Island, one of the smaller of the group.

"One leaves the mainland," she wrote me, "and trouble is left behind. The world is forgotten, and the clean air sweeps one to absolute ecstasy."

Mrs. Single has traced the history of the Thimbles back to their purchase from the Indians by a group of Puritan emigrants from Massachusetts. The deal was unusual because the Indian side was handled by a squaw. She apparently later regretted the bargain she had made and committed suicide. In 1700 the ubiquitous Captain William Kidd is supposed to have buried treasure on Money Island, a supposition which gives the island its name. In 1924 a visitor to the island did find a remarkable ring which dates at least as far back as the sixteenth century and has been valued at two thousand dollars, far better evidence than most treasure trove legends have to back them up.

Nowadays, according to Mrs. Single, the islands are summer homes exclusively. A few intrepid souls visit them occasionally from March to November, but May to September is the season for most families. Groceries and other supplies are delivered by boat from Stony Creek, and whenever anyone tries to ferry across some large item in a small boat, the whole island population pitches in, at least with advice. Years ago one islander created for himself among staid Stony Creekers a permanent reputation as a madcap by ferrying across a piano and playing it as he went.

A few of the wealthier islands have city power, telephones and water piped from the mainland. "But," as Mrs. Single puts it, "everyone else uses kerosene lamps and likes the primitive look and the care of them. At night they make a soft glow of light from the cottages, really quite a wonderful sight." Most, however, do have bottled gas for cooking and refrigeration, and excellent wells provide good plumbing facilities.

During the summer a few heads of families commute daily or on week ends from as far away as New York, but many of the islanders don't go ashore for months on end. There is good clamming and fishing and they have frequent clambakes. Swimming is excellent, and there are rock cliffs on some of the islands for high diving. Most of the islanders do their own carpentering and painting.

"There's usually a breeze," Mrs. Single says, "and squalls can spring up with little warning. When they do, everyone rushes to batten down the hatches and make everything tight. Boats get double lines, and we keep an anxious eye on all the harbor craft. Sometimes the storms pass as quickly as they come, but when a northeaster or a line storm hits, we just bring in plenty of wood and settle down to enjoy a quiet three days' rest at home."

Some of the cottages are rented out every summer at, Mrs. Single told me, reasonable prices. A few are occasionally for sale. But the only two reported to me as definitely for sale recently were scarcely cottages. One was a ten-acre portion with half a mile of waterfront on one of the larger Thimble Islands. It had a nineteen-room main house in the half-timbered style, an eight-room caretaker's house, a boathouse, a tennis court and various other trimmings, and the asking price was seventy thousand dollars. Another was an entire four-acre island with a fifteen-room main house, a seven-room guest cottage, a boathouse, and another boathouse on the mainland; the asking price was fifty thousand dollars.

Many of the other Connecticut islands westward toward New York are in the same or even higher price brackets. A few are in the "estate development" class, and homes on them might occasionally be available in the fifteen- to thirty-thousand-dollar range. But more typical is Bartram's Island near Stamford, which changed hands a few years ago for a hundred thousand.

Ed and Pegeen Fitzgerald, the radio breakfast program couple, are enthusiastic owners of Hay Island near Darien. About fifteen acres in area, it is connected to the mainland by a causeway which is submerged by the highest tides. The Fitzgeralds spend most of their time there the year round, although they also keep an apartment in New York City.

"We had to have an island," Ed Fitzgerald told me, "because of the animals. They just don't understand about property lines."

Animals are a sort of trade mark for the Fitzgeralds. They regularly give shelter to pets which their friends or members of their radio audience have to part with. Whoever might have been their neighbor if they hadn't bought the island should give daily thanks that they did buy it, unless he is a deeply devoted animal lover, too. When I was there, I counted eleven dogs ranging from a Scotty to a great Dane, forty-eight cats and kittens, a deer, a goose and a goat. From the sounds which emanated from various outbuildings, I judged I hadn't seen the half of it.

The Fitzgeralds have one good tip for other owners of coastal islands — namely, build well back from the water's edge. Their house is only about fifty feet inland, and two winters of salt spray so pitted the windows facing the sea that they were completely opaque. They also warn that you can expect just about anything to wash up on your shores. A frisky, five-hundred-pound porpoise once leaped onto their beach and expired. They could find no one who would take it away and had to bury it at considerable expense. But they also find all the firewood they can use, and they have eight fireplaces.

## New York

There are four separate groups of islands along the New York coast: (1) in the southwestern end of Long Island Sound along the shores of Westchester and the upper Bronx; (2) in the East River and New York Bay; (3) off the eastern tip of Long Island; (4) along the southern, seaward shore of Long Island.

(1) Most of Westchester's islands are close inshore and are connected to the mainland by causeways. Since they are all within easy commuting range of midtown Manhattan, property on them is in great demand and expensive. A typical one is North Manursing Island off Rye, from which it is only thirty-five minutes to Grand Central Station. A contractor took it over not long after World War II and built several houses, on which he put such price tags as $78,500 and $80,000. The price on bare building sites was $8500 each.

The islands off the Bronx at the end of Long Island Sound mostly either are parts of Pelham Bay Park or are heavily built up. City Island, a big yachting and seafood center, has a population of forty-five hundred. Some of the others have armed forces installations.

Until shortly before World War II one tiny island, just off Pelham Bay Park, afforded a way of life unique among islands in this area. It was inhabited by a small group of determinedly Bohemian escapees from Greenwich Village, who lived there the way Villagers are supposed to live, according to legend, but seldom do in reality. They solved the water problem chiefly by ignoring it in favor of beer. But such freedom was too good to last and came to an abrupt end when the municipal government expropriated the island.

(2) Of New York City's five boroughs only the Bronx is on the mainland. Brooklyn and Queens share the western

tip of Long Island, Staten Island makes up the borough of Richmond, and Manhattan Island is the borough of Manhattan. In addition, there are a dozen small islands scattered along the East River and in New York Bay. Most have city or Federal installations of one kind or another, such as Rikers Island with its city jail, Governors Island with Fort Jay, and Ellis Island with its Immigration Service headquarters. Thirteen people — four employees of the National Park Service and their families — have homes on Bedloes Island beneath the Statue of Liberty.

Far out in the bay are two small islands which would make still more unusual homes if they ever become available for that purpose. They are Hoffman Island and Swinburne Island in the area where Lower New York Bay shades into the Atlantic Ocean. Originally mere rocks, they were built up with gravel and concrete fill in 1872 to serve as quarantine stations for some of the thousands of immigrants then pouring into the country. When the stream of immigrants dried to a trickle in the 1920's, the Immigration Service moved out, and the islands have since been used only occasionally for such purposes as training merchant marine engine crews during World War II.

Now they look like deserted villages, the buildings standing empty and with many windows broken by the occasional vandals who are almost the only visitors. According to one story there are vaults full of funeral urns on Swinburne. It seems that there was an outbreak of bubonic plague among one group of immigrants, and bodies of the victims were cremated and their ashes stored on the island. This probably would make for a plethora of ghosts. In any case the islands are now under the authority of the Public Buildings Administration, which has classified them as "frozen," meaning that they are not for sale, at least for the time being.

But there are genuine private island hideaways well within the city limits. They are in Jamaica Bay on the southern, seaward side of the Long Island tip. Scattered over the bay, which lies half in Brooklyn and half in Queens, are more than a hundred islands, varying in size from a fraction of an acre to a square mile or more. Most are mere marshy sand spits, but at least two provide summer havens for several of New York's most fortunate though by no means wealthiest families.

Back around the turn of the century before the shallow water of the bay was befouled by sewage and industrial waste, there were great oyster and clam beds among these islands "farmed" by families who lived there the year round. Some of the descendants of those families, who had to look elsewhere for a way to earn a living long ago, still own cottages on Ruffle Bar and Pumpkin Patch Islands and commute to them from Brooklyn or Manhattan during the summer. Only occasionally do any of the families spend the year round there now, but from late spring to early fall they have exactly what the hordes of other New Yorkers who rush back and forth along the highways ringing the bay are seeking and seldom finding. The only drawback is that small boys sometimes chance on the islands during the winter and find the opportunity for destruction irresistible. Sooner or later someone will start "developing" the islands, but for the time being they offer a chance for scot-free escape.

(3) Some hundred miles to the east off the opposite end of Long Island are half a dozen widely varied islands. Two of these, Plum Island and Great Gull Island, were among the bargains offered for sale by the War Assets Administration. As usual, the W.A.A. offer was deceptive, in these cases almost cruelly so. Various would-be islanders offered bids ranging as high as eighty-five thousand dollars. After keeping

them on tenterhooks for several months the Army decided to retain Plum Island, and the W.A.A. presented Great Gull Island to the American Museum of Natural History as a gift.

Nearby Gardiners Island is one of the nation's oldest pieces of real estate under the continuous ownership of a single family. The royal grant of the island to the original Gardiner was made in 1639, and it specified entailment, meaning that it could not be sold out of the family but must be passed on intact from each generation to the next. A house and slave quarters on it date back to pre-Revolutionary War days, but the main building is a twenty-eight-room mansion built since World War II. The island currently is rented to a wealthy sportsman who uses it chiefly as a private hunting ground.

Far out in the open water to the northeast, so far that ferry service to it is from New London, Connecticut, rather than from Long Island, is Fishers Island. It is on the dividing line between Long Island Sound and Block Island Sound and has a reputation for being what the state publicity men call a "high-type summer resort colony." This means that many of its inhabitants are in the yacht-owning class. One forty-seven-acre property on it which was sold to a St. Louis woman a few years ago had a price tag of forty-five thousand dollars.

Shelter Island, on the other hand, is a "sport fishing and tourist resort summer colony." Lying between the two arms of Long Island, which splits apart at its eastern end, Shelter Island has a year-round population of a thousand or more and a huge influx of vacationers in the summer. But it is possible to find cottages with nearly complete privacy and something of the island feelings. Rents start as low as thirty dollars or so per week.

(4) From a few hundred feet to as much as six miles out in the open Atlantic off Long Island's south shore lie four long, narrow islands. The first starts at a point near the

New York City limits, and the last reaches almost to the end of Long Island. Three are known only by the names of their beaches — Long Beach, the nearest to New York City, Jones Beach, the second one out, and Westhampton Beach, the furthest from the city. These three are connected to Long Island by bridges and traversed from end to end by roads so that they don't really permit much of an escape from civilization. Long Beach, in fact, is as solidly built up as most cities.

But the fourth one, Fire Island, is one of the best of bets for anyone seeking an island home in the New York City area. Lying three or four miles offshore for most of its length, it stretches for about thirty miles from a point opposite Babylon, Long Island, to a point opposite East Moriches. In many places it is only a quarter of a mile wide and it is nowhere more than a mile across, so that in spite of its length you are always aware that you are surrounded by water.

A state park occupies about four miles of the western end nearest New York City, and there are several big colonies of summer homes plus a few year-round inhabitants scattered along the next ten miles to the east. But even in this part of the island you can get off by yourself, and farther east there are many miles of open country. You reach the island via small ferries from Bay Shore or Patchogue, and once there you either walk or take a jeep taxi along the beach. No roads encumber the island.

In the last few years congenial groups of New Yorkers have been building colonies of cottages at wide intervals along the eastward stretches. Among the most successful of these groups is one to which a young couple who are friends of mine belong. After renting a cottage for several summers, at five hundred dollars or more per Memorial Day to Labor Day season, they decided in 1950 to build their own. Since, like many islanders, they don't want publicity, I'll call them Peter and Marie Smith.

The Smiths bought a plot one hundred feet by seventy-five feet near the center of the island where several other couples were building. It came to about $670 altogether, including survey and title search fees and such sundries. Though he had no drafting experience at all, Peter worked out a neat design for a three-bedroom, living room, kitchen and bath cottage with a flat roof for use as a sun deck. He found a carpenter who, with his help, put up the shell of the building for a little over three thousand dollars. Peter and Marie and assorted friends lured with promises of future week-end invitations took over from there. The result is a pleasant and wonderfully comfortable cottage at a total outlay, including land, of a little over four thousand dollars.

Three discoveries made by the Smiths can be very helpful to other island cottage builders. One is a one-manpower pile driver for driving wells in sandy soil. It is simply a weight with which you can pound lengths of pipe into the sand, the first length being sharply pointed and perforated. The perforations are screened with closely meshed copper to keep out the sand and let in the water. It worked so well for Peter that he dug two wells in case one should go dry. It wouldn't work so well, of course, in rocky or tightly packed clay soil.

The second Smith discovery was a solution for the bedding problem. Many islands, including Fire Island, have a great deal of damp weather which rusts bedsprings and makes ordinary mattresses musty and sour. The Smiths made beds of plain wooden platforms and covered them with unsheathed foam rubber. So far they have served their purpose perfectly.

The third helpful hint concerns the floor finish. On a sandy island, unless you apply rigid and joyless discipline to your family and your guests, they are bound to track quantities of sand into the house. With ordinary floors, sweeping it out is an endless and difficult job. So the experimentally minded Smiths tried applying three coats of deck enamel to their floors. The result is a smooth, uncracked finish, and the sand can be swept out almost as easily as it is tracked in.

It ought to take at least another generation or two for Fire Island to reach the "development" stage. If you want to plan beyond that, there are a few dozen small islands in Great South Bay, which lies between Fire Island and Long Island, and in Moriches Bay to the east and South Oyster Bay to the west. Like the islands of Jamaica Bay within the New York City limits, they are low, sandy and often marshy. But summer homes have been built on many of them, and there are others not yet built on which would be suitable. They lack the ocean surf which is one of the chief attractions of Fire Island, but most of them are safe against the inroads of civilization in any foreseeable future.

## New Jersey

Like the seaward side of Long Island, most of the coast of New Jersey from Point Pleasant south to Cape May is lined with long, narrow islands and peninsulas of sand. But all of these islands are connected with the mainland by bridges and are traversed by highways. Most of them have beach resorts scattered at frequent intervals along their entire lengths. Absecon Island, for instance, is almost completely built up, with Atlantic City at one end plus the towns of Ventnor, Margate City and Longport.

Between these big islands and the mainland, however, are a number of bays and harbors dotted with hundreds of islets. The great majority are low, marshy spits of sand on which sedge grass is the only vegetation. Some are built up one year and washed away the next by the action of the tides. The more stable of some of the lowest ones are maintained by groups of hunters for duck hunting in the fall, but they are useful for little else.

There are a number of higher and dryer islands on which Philadelphians and New Jerseyites have summer homes. One group is used as a summer classroom by teachers and students from a Philadelphia art school. And some can be used as year-round homes, as one remarkable hermit has proved beyond dispute.

This man, Alfred Conover, was officially counted as part of the population of the United States for the first time in the census of 1950. He was then seventy-eight years old. It took remarkable persistence on the part of a census enumerator to get him counted, too.

Conover's counting began when the enumerator heard from residents of Atlantic City's outskirts that "some old guy lives out there on one of those islands, we think." But these particular islands are set in the midst of salt marshes too shallow and weedy for ordinary motorboats. The enumerator tried rowing but gave up exhausted after a couple of miles, still far short of his goal. Finally, after three weeks of frustration, the enumerator got the co-operation of the United States Navy, which dispatched a shallow-draft fireboat to aid him. When they finally tracked down Conover, the old gentleman was less pleased than surprised to see them.

"Nobody ever got out here before," he allowed. "I've been on this island since I came here with my pa, fifty years ago."

This, I think, makes Conover the nation's all-time champion island escapee. He lives mostly on fish, plus what he can buy with the proceeds from occasional catches which he rows into Atlantic City to sell. If you want to go and do likewise, you will find plenty of choice of island retreats like his along the Jersey coast.

If you are not quite so determined to get away from everything, or if you don't have a constitution of the high iron content necessary, you will also find a fair range of choice among more nearly civilized, or at least civilizable, islands there. One reported to me as definitely for sale is just offshore near the Wildwood resort a few miles north of Cape May. It's about half a mile long and a quarter-mile wide at the widest and has no buildings. Because of its close proximity to the resort town, the asking price is a stiff seven thousand dollars.

But many others have more privacy and would come far cheaper if you can find the owner in the selling mood. That requires on-the-spot exploration. The best way to undertake this, and a fine cruise in itself, is to sail or motorboat along the Inland Waterway, which threads among these islands down most of the length of the state's coast.

## Maryland and Virginia

Delaware Bay and the Atlantic coast of Delaware have few islands and none of much interest, but the Eastern Shore of Maryland and Virginia, the long peninsula jutting south between the Atlantic and Chesapeake Bay, is island-rich. There are at least fifty, and perhaps twice that many, along the Atlantic sides of the two states and an equal or greater number in Chesapeake Bay. No official of either state would commit himself beyond saying that the total is "large." I'm lumping the two states together because their islands are closely intermingled and much alike.

Along most of the length of the Atlantic side of the Eastern Shore runs a series of long, low, narrow islands like those off Long Island and New Jersey. Only one, Chincoteague, which has over three thousand inhabitants, is heavily populated. It caters chiefly to the serious fisherman sort of tourist who goes there for Hemingwayesque battles with marlin.

Chincoteague and nearby Assateague share the much publicized mystery ponies. These are stunted horses, averaging about four and a half feet in height, which run wild on the islands except for an annual roundup and branding of foals when a few are auctioned off to visitors. The big mystery concerns their origin. Supposedly there are none like them anywhere else on earth. One faction insists that they are the remnant of hordes of prehistoric horses which roamed the continent until they were nearly wiped out by disease. Another romantic theory traces them to a pirate crew which may have used the island as a base in the seventeenth century and abandoned a few horses in making a hasty departure. They grew stunted, according to this explanation, because they couldn't get enough to eat on the islands.

Around the peninsula in Chesapeake Bay are Tangier and Smith Islands, whose human inhabitants have long been far more interestingly mysterious than the Chincoteague ponies. Smith Islanders trace their lineage back to the members of Captain John Smith's company who settled there nearly three hundred years ago, and most Tangier families have lived on their island for a similar period. Until the last generation they resisted all attempts at modernization and reportedly clung even to seventeenth-century word pronunciations and turns of phrase. They still live, as they always have, by oystering, crabbing and fishing, and according to the town clerk of Tangier, "We have no bathrooms except in a few isolated cases." Electric power crept in only five years ago.

A few of the other Eastern Shore islands have similar, though less completely isolated, communities. Many are owned and used as retreats by city people, mostly from Washington,

Baltimore, Wilmington, Philadelphia and New York. Unfortunately, the local real-estate dealers I talked to take little interest in island properties. The chief reason for this is that the islands are so widely scattered that the dealers can't afford to give them much attention. Only one of them reported an island definitely for sale.

This was thirteen-acre St. Helena Island in the mouth of the Severn River ten miles from Annapolis. It had a large Colonial mansion, several outbuildings, a hothouse, a deer park, a good wharf and extensive landscaping. According to the dealer, the former owner had spent more than three hundred thousand dollars on it, and it was being offered for sale to close the estate. The asking price was seventy-five thousand dollars.

Other informants tell me that there are islands in Chesapeake Bay and along the coast which "probably" could be had for a fraction of this amount, but no one could be specific. There are a few islands in the public domain, though, which can be had for nothing — while they last. The trouble is that they may last only a few weeks or months. These are sand bars which constantly are being built up and torn down by tidal action. Several of them have been granted by the Maryland Land Office to lucky duck hunters, but no one has thought of any other use for them.

## Sources of Additional Information

CONNECTICUT

*Real-Estate Dealers*

Kusterer Brothers, Inc.
129 Church Street
New Haven, Connecticut

Previews, Inc.
49 East 53rd Street
New York 22, New York

## NEW YORK
### *General*
Fire Island Chamber of Commerce
Fire Island, New York

Shelter Island, Chamber of Commerce
Shelter Island, New York

### *Real-Estate Dealers*
Shelter Island:
Griffing & Collins
Shelter Island, New York

Fishers Island:
Franklin Haines
Fishers Island
c/o Postmaster
New London, Connecticut

## NEW JERSEY, MARYLAND AND VIRGINIA
United States Coast and Geodetic Survey
Department of Commerce
Washington 25, D. C.
(For charts of the Inland Waterway.)

CHAPTER VIII

## South Sea Islands—North Carolina to Texas

ALONG THE COASTS of the southeastern United States stretch large numbers of widely varied islands, most of which will give you a chance at the languorous, seagirt sort of life usually associated with the islands of the South Pacific. At best, of course, they are only semitropical, and there are no Polynesian maidens to welcome you with garlands of flowers. But you can, if you want to, get by on many of them with little more than a palm-thatched-hut type of shelter and a reasonable approximation of a beachcomber's indolence.

They include the Atlantic islands from North Carolina south to the Florida Keys, and all those in the great arc of the Gulf of Mexico from the Everglades around to Brownsville, Texas. Taking North Carolina as the starting point is a little arbitrary since its climate isn't much warmer than that of Chesapeake Bay. But the state is the northern limit of the wild palm's extent, and palm trees seem to me essential to the tropical or even semitropical mood.

Altogether there are at least several thousand habitable islands along this stretch of coast. The total is many times that number if swamps and shifting sand bars are included. A few of the desirable ones still are in the public domain and available, under some circumstances, to private citizens, the only American islands of which this is true. But the great majority are privately owned.

## North Carolina

Off most of the coast of North Carolina the chain of long, narrow, sandy islands found further north repeats itself. One group of these is in the form of an arrowhead pointing out to sea with the point, Cape Hatteras, some thirty miles out from the mainland. Scattered here and there along most of them are fishing villages and resorts. Some are so heavily built up that you are seldom out of sight of cottages, but there are long empty stretches on others where building sites can be had at what I'm told are "reasonable" prices.

Behind the protecting sweep of the Outer Banks, as these islands are called, lie Pamlico Sound, Albemarle Sound, Currituck Sound and several other lagoonlike and comparatively shallow bodies of water. Several large islands are scattered among them. One is Roanoke Island, where Sir Walter Raleigh established the first British colony in North America and where Paul Green's play about the colony is presented every summer. Roanoke is thickly populated, but some of the other big Sound islands, such as Durant Island, consist of large and fertile farms.

To escape-minded city dwellers a farm often seems like the ideal haven of peace and quiet. An island farm is doubly so. With such a habitat you can cut yourself off from the rest of the world completely, if you want to work at it. A number of the islanders in the North Carolina sounds have succeeded in the project so well that all I could learn about them is that they exist.

Some of the smaller islands are used chiefly as hunting lodges. The late Joseph Knapp, a publicity-shy New York multimillionaire owned one of these — Mackey's Island in Currituck Sound near the Dismal Swamp. But they are not all in the millionaire class. This is fortunate since Currituck (an Indian word meaning wild geese) has some of the nation's best waterfowl hunting.

A few of the islands in Albemarle and Pamlico Sounds are the undependable kind. The Outer Banks don't filter out all the force of the storms which occasionally lash the coast, and when the weather is running heavy, huge chunks of the inner islands sometimes wash away. Years ago a man named Batt owned an island of twenty-seven acres. The one acre which is all that's left is known as Batts Grave because he disappeared from it along with part of his island in a storm.

Smith Island (also known as Bald Head), near the southern end of the state, reportedly "might" be for sale in whole or in part. Some seventeen thousand acres in extent, it lies four miles out to sea off Southport. It has a lighthouse and keeper's cottage on the seaward point, but the only other permanent inhabitants are wild pigs and small game. Part of it is densely wooded with palmetto, hickory, dogwood and live oak. With the Gulf Stream passing only a few miles away, it is frost-free and, according to local sportsmen, an ideal fishing base.

## South Carolina

South Carolina's coastal islands, according to a man who has spent his life among them, number "goodness knows how many," meaning at least several hundred. On some there are dense tropical growths to rival any equatorial jungle, and several are more like swamps than islands. But there are many which are quite habitable, and in general they are smaller and more private than most of those in North Carolina. They are also closer inshore, often being separated from the mainland and from each other only by narrow, winding inlets.

Some of the smallest ones seem to be forgotten property. Their owners, if any, never visit them or use them for any purpose. A few such may not belong to anyone, though it would take extensive and expensive research to establish this.

But most of the desirable ones are old-time plantations. Some of these have been broken up into farms by descendants of the slaves who worked them before Emancipation and who speak the half-English, half-Bantu dialect called Gullah. Others have been put to some odd uses. One of these was for some time a nudist colony. Another was a rendezvous for bootleggers and rumrunners during Prohibition days, but at last report its population was down to one hermit.

A few such island plantations have been restored to their old elegance at great expense during the last generation. One near Beaufort was offered for sale recently. It covers six hundred acres, of which five are beautifully landscaped and the rest woodland and "high marsh." It has a plantation house with the traditional pillars plus an indoor swimming pool, an outlandish feature in an island home, and two guest cottages. The asking price was a hundred thousand dollars.

Three other larger ones near Charleston have been for sale at prices not reported to me. One of the most interesting of these lies three miles offshore and is three and a half miles long by a mile and a half wide. It supports not only deer and other ordinary game but also wild cattle, sheep and pigs. Miles of sandy beach line the seaward side, and several fresh-water ponds guarantee the water supply. Oysters, clams and crabs are plentiful. Occasionally, huge sea turtles turn up on the beach to lay their eggs. A group of Audubon Society observers once counted 141 species of birds, including wild turkeys. It sounds like a wilderness paradise.

## *Georgia*

Off Georgia's hundred miles of coast lie seventy-five islands by the count of the Brunswick Chamber of Commerce, which considers them one of its chief attractions. They are sometimes known as the Golden Isles of Guale (pronounced "wallie"), and the term "golden" taken in its financial sense is well deserved. Several of them are among the most expensively luxurious estates still extant in this country. And Sea Island has The Cloister, a resort hotel whose tone you can judge from the fact that it puts out for prospective guests a booklet entitled "What to Wear at Sea Island."

Fine sand beaches line the seaward sides of nearly all the islands, and their soil is rich. Where the junglelike growth has been cleared, the owners raise nearly all northern vegetables and fruits plus figs, persimmons, pecans, rice and sugar cane. You can find all the usual fish and shellfish plus such rarities as terrapin. Some of the islands have deer, and there are usually quail, snipe and waterfowl on all of them.

One of the largest is St. Catherine's Island, ten miles long and four wide. Edward J. Noble, who also owns several of the Thousand Islands, bought it in 1943 for a winter home. Being no man to waste anything, he has started timbering and turpentine operations among the pine forests which cover most of the island and also runs several hundred head of beef cattle. These two undertakings would be possible on many of the other Georgia islands and, in the current state of the market for both products, could make them self-sustaining.

But the only one of the larger ones which changed hands recently carried a purchase price of $675,000. This was Jekyll Island, and the purchaser was the state government. Back in 1886 the island had been acquired by a group of a hundred of the nation's wealthiest families — Morgans, Rockefellers, Goulds and such. They built homes (J. P. Morgan regally and unself-consciously named his Sans Souci after the palace built by Frederick the Great of Prussia), and made it rigidly exclusive. But their descendants couldn't meet the upkeep costs. Neither, it developed, could the State of Georgia. After trying for a couple of years to make it a state park, the state government gave up and leased it to a hotel for use as a private resort.

One of the smaller islands near Savannah, Oatland Island, is a United States Public Health Service laboratory for studies of communicable disease. The island proved ideal for such studies and started a trend toward the use of other islands for similar purposes by the Department of Agriculture and other agencies.

There are a few Georgia islands in the private class which fall below the millionaire level in cost. A Massachusetts couple bought one near the South Carolina border in the early thirties, made it self-sustaining, and raised a large family of youngsters who seldom even visited the mainland before they went off to college. If you can't or don't want to spend large sums, though, your best bet in this area is to rent a home on one of the larger islands.

### Florida

Thousands of islands ring the Florida coasts and stretch out to the south toward Key West and the Dry Tortugas. Many, as the last named group indicates, are desert islands, and many are mangrove swamps. But others are either already quite habitable or could be made so.

The State of Florida still owns a good many of the islands. Until a couple of years ago it maintained a strict "no sale" policy. Now, however, it is willing to entertain bids and is selling, one official told me, "quite a number" of islands.

Most of those sold have been four acres or less in area. Prices have ranged from a hundred dollars per acre to more than two thousand, the cheaper ones usually being swampy and requiring expensive reclamation work to make them habitable. In addition, the state leases island camp sites at about fifty dollars per acre per year.

The chief catch is that you must find the island yourself and establish the fact that the state owns it before you can even submit a bid. No records have been kept or surveys made of any of them, and they are scattered widely along both coasts of the state. Consequently, the best I can do is describe the various types of islands, among which there are many privately owned as well as those belonging to the state. I'll begin with the east coast, swing south through the Keys and back north along the west coast.

The series of long, low, sandy islands which begins off New York's Long Island continues along Florida's east coast, but many of these have been developed as resorts. Palm Beach is one such. Consequently, island properties come high. One group of three small ones within the city limits of Fort Lauderdale was offered a couple of years ago for two hundred thousand dollars. And single lots on the heavily built up islands in Biscayne Bay off Miami cost from eight to fifteen thousand dollars each.

There are a few comparatively private stretches on some of the larger east coast islands and some desirable small islands in the bays and lagoons cut off from the sea by the long ones.

The Inland Waterway, which winds among these protected waters, offers a fine way of exploring. But you will find a much wider choice among the Keys to the south and along the Gulf coast.

The Overseas Highway, which runs for 122 miles in a southwesterly arc from the southern tip of the Florida mainland to Key West, links thirty-nine of the Keys. Nowhere will you find an easier way of reaching a sea island. But the highway, of course, cuts down the privacy of those islands it touches. Fortunately, there are plenty of others. The Keys total, according to which authority you heed, either seven hundred or about eight hundred.

Along with the privacy you can find away from the highway Keys goes a difficult water problem. Flowing wells are rare, and the big Keys get the greater part of their water by pipeline from the mainland. Most of the owners of islands off the highway solve the problem more or less satisfactorily by building wide, flat roofs and collecting rain water. But in long dry spells they sometimes have to ferry cask loads from the highway.

Chiefly for this reason several otherwise quite attractive islands are unoccupied. On the other hand, many dreamers of island dreams have been undaunted by such troubles. Among the most determined and most successful have been Captain and Mrs. Percy A. Cook. A descendant of Captain James Cook, the explorer who discovered Australia, the present Captain Cook was born in England seventy years ago and spent most of the early part of his life knocking around the world in a highly romantic fashion, even doing a little exploring of his own in Africa. By the early 1920's he had settled down in Scotch Plains, New Jersey, to a business of manufacturing remedies for poultry diseases. But he had long since made up his mind that what he wanted more than anything else was an island of his own. Mrs. Cook shared his enthusiasm for the idea. It was on a winter trip to Florida in 1922 that they heard one of the small Keys was for sale, took a look at it and bought it on the spot.

"My friends," the captain told me, "thought I had gone nuts. But they changed their minds a couple of years later when I turned down two separate offers of thirty times what I had payed for it. We still won't take any amount of money for it. It's paradise to us, and with all the money in the world we couldn't buy anything better."

Nowadays the Cooks spend five months of the year in Scotch Plains and the rest on Cook Island, as they have named their paradise. It covers some fifty acres but is so irregular in shape that the total shoreline is nearly five miles in length, including several long stretches of magnificent beach. The location is two miles off Big Pine Key on the Atlantic side and five miles from the Overseas Highway.

Much of the island is covered by dense tropical growth which includes fine stands of coconut palms, date palms, avocado and papaya trees. A thick layer of leaf mold covers the basic coral sand and makes it possible to grow almost anything. A submerged reef surrounds most of the island and takes the force of the sea so that even in a gale a skiff can lie at its mooring without danger. In addition, the reef provides protection for rock lobster, stone crabs and conches, so that they are always handy when wanted.

In their thirty years on the island the warmest temperature the Cooks have recorded was 89° and the coldest 52°. The average top through the winter is 78° and the bottom 65°. There have been winters without a single day of rain, and seldom has there been more than a few days of it. A heavy dew which falls most nights provides all the moisture the island needs.

Water supplies have never been a problem for the Cooks, even at the beginning when they had only a small galvanized iron roof on their cottage and a single thousand-gallon tank. Now they have an extensive system of iron and aluminum water-collecting systems, five-thousand-gallon tanks, a ten-thousand-gallon cement cistern, and a five-hundred-gallon tank on stilts which provides hot water with the help of the sun's heat.

During the first years the captain used windmills to generate electricity and recommends them highly, since there usually is a sea breeze blowing among the Keys. But he has graduated to a Diesel because there usually are so many guests around that he needs more electricity than the windmills could provide. Bottled gas and kerosene provide cooking heat and run the refrigerators.

Mosquitoes and other insect plagues endemic to the tropics don't concern the Cooks much. Sometimes, largely as a result of the steady breeze, they don't see a single insect from November to May. When some do turn up, a little spraying and occasional use of repellents keeps them under control. Sand flies turn up during dead calm periods but are kept out of the house by screens sprayed with repellents. And in thirty years the captain has seen only two snakes on the island, and he shot both of those.

When he bought the island, there were no buildings of any kind, and the growth was so dense that he had to hack his way through with a machete. Since then, doing most of the work himself with occasional help from guests, he has built a main house and three cottages for guests. During most of the winter there are from two to a dozen of the latter on hand. Without them the captain estimates that he and his wife could live quite comfortably on the island for as little as a hundred dollars a month.

"But," he adds, "if you own an island paradise, you can be sure you will have guests. Anyway, we want to have them. They always want to pay, but we are quite determined not to let them."

He built his main house on stilts to get the cooling and drying effect from breezes moving freely under it. Another result is a magnificent view from the wide veranda around it. Reclining on it and gazing out over waving palm fronds to the deep blue Gulf Stream, the Cooks and their fortunate guests make a picture closer to the South Sea island ideal than you probably could find in the South Seas themselves.

Even hurricanes don't mar the picture according to the captain. Several have passed over the island and have done little damage because, as he puts it, he "built for them." The only important harm was done when four coconut palms blew over onto the roof of the main house a couple of years ago. But he insists that this was his fault because he planted the trees too close to the house.

You won't find anything like Cook Island for sale cheap among the Keys or, for that matter, anywhere else. It is the result of thirty years of hard and loving work. But there are many still in the condition in which the Cooks found theirs in 1923. Key real estate, however, is in the midst of a minor boom, and you will have to go far off the Overseas Highway chain to find any whole islands very cheap unless you can turn up a state-owned island and obtain a lease on it.

Dealers in Key real estate told me of several currently for sale. They ranged from eight acres up to 213 acres. But because of the growing popularity of the Keys and consequent rise in property values, I could get a definite asking price on only one. This was seventy-five hundred dollars for a two-hundred-acre portion of one of the big Keys some thirty miles north of Key West.

Among the lucky few who have found real bargains in Key properties recently were a group of forty-five ex-G.I.'s and their families. In the fall of 1949 the United States Bureau of Land Management announced that it was ready to sell forty-five lots of about two acres each on Saddle Bunch Key, and that veterans would receive preference. More than sixteen hundred sent in applications. The forty-five whose applications were accepted got their lots for only nominal payments plus agreements to make improvements.

Incidentally, the Bureau of Land Management says that this probably is the last island property it will offer for sale. The publicity resulting from this sale resulted in a deluge of queries. The Bureau's reply to all was: "The few remaining islands in the public [federal] domain often are inaccessible masses of rock not classified for disposal, or are otherwise unavailable to seekers of vacation spots [see Appendix II]."

If you are willing to make the sacrifice of privacy (along with the sacrifice, of course, goes a gain in convenience) of having the Overseas Highway near at hand, there are many developments under way on Keys crossed by the highway. You will have neighbors close by. But you can count on their help in controlling mosquitoes. (As the Cooks have found, these are not too troublesome during the winter, but if you plan to stay through the summer you may find them one of your chief problems.)

The highway makes the Keys the easiest to explore of any large island group I have found. Key West at the end of the highway is a booming resort town, partly as a result of the publicity focused on it by President Truman's visits, and you will find tourist cottages which make excellent bases for exploration scattered all the way along, with fair-sized concentrations of them at Tavernier and Marathon. And there are numerous real-estate dealers to help you in your search.

Like most coastal islands, the Keys have their legends of treasure. But in this case there is indisputable truth to at least one of them. A couple of years ago a professional deep-sea diver named Arthur McKee was making underwater movies off Long Key and stumbled on the remains of a genuine Spanish galleon. He even found bars of silver treasure. But silver is no longer quite the treasure it once was. McKee is cashing in on his find in the hardheaded modern business-man's way of organizing a sunken treasure museum and reg-ular tourist excursions to the site of the wreckage.

Northeast of the Keys stretches Florida's Gulf coast and the largest group of islands in the United States. According to a Saint Petersburg enthusiast: "There are at least half a million ranging in size from a mere dot of sand topped by mangroves to several hundred acres. Probably 99 per cent of them are uninhabited, not because they are uninhabitable but because this part of the state of Florida is still in a frontier condition."

This sounds to me a bit overenthusiastic. But no one ever has counted the islands, and it is impossible to be more specific than to say that there must be more than a hundred thousand of them. It's quite true that only a sparse few near the bigger towns have been developed in any way and that the rest form a sort of by-passed frontier. But it's also true that many will probably stay that way permanently because they are too swampy for any foreseeable use.

Even the higher and drier islands have disadvantages in some cases. On some of them rattlers and other snakes are fairly numerous, though probably not much more so than in the northern woods. Mosquitoes, roaches and other insects can be troublesome on others, particularly during the summer. And wells sometimes yield only brackish water which is suit-able for washing but undrinkable, so that you must either import your drinking water or depend on rain water collection.

But that's enough about the drawbacks. The attractions are far more than enough to balance them, and there are many among these islands which present none of these problems. For a moonlight night on a white sand beach all your own, palm trees whispering gently overhead, the warm sea splashing phosphorescently, the wonderful, mysterious smell of the tropics in the air — in return for all this you probably would find it possible to put up with far more serious difficulties.

The islands along the southwestern tip of the Florida coast are part of Everglades National Park and, of course, are not for sale, rent or other private use. But just north of the Everglades boundary lie the Ten Thousand Islands. Local people insist that the name for the group is an understatement. The great majority are too low and swampy to be of much use, but that still leaves a large number to choose among.

Some of those near the northern edge of the group are comparatively well tamed, with a few tiny villages scattered here and there among them and regular ferry service from the mainland. But if you want to test your mettle under frontier conditions subtropical style, you can find them unsoftened to the south. Until the last generation the maze of islands was a haven for outlaws, and it probably still harbors occasional fugitives. One of the most colorful characters in its past was "Emperor" Ed Watson, who ruled it murderously for many years around the turn of the century. He ran several sugar plantations on various islands with the labor of other bad men whom he impressed into his service, and once he reportedly put to work a sheriff who came in from outside to attempt to arrest him. In 1910 his employees finally plucked up their courage and shot him, then hanged his body just to make sure.

Many of the islands in the group are owned by a company

founded by the late Barron Collier, an advertising tycoon who dreamed of turning the region into a great resort. A number of properties have been listed for sale recently. They range from building lots at $450 apiece on one of the more thickly settled islands to a mile-long stretch of magnificent beach connected to the mainland by a causeway and hopefully touted as "ideal for development" at an asking price of $115,000. In between are whole islands and parts of larger ones, ranging from ten to a hundred or more acres, at three to eleven thousand dollars each.

From the Ten Thousand Islands north to Tampa Bay the coast is thickly lined with islands. (Many of the smaller ones are called keys, a word deriving from the Spanish *cayo*, which means "small island." Since to most people *the* Florida Keys are the group stretching out to sea off the southern tip of the state, I have capitalized the word in referring to them and will spell it with a small letter in referring to those of the Gulf coast.) Scattered among them are many luxurious and expensive estates, but hundreds of others are well within range of almost everyone's pocketbook.

Off Fort Myers lie several big islands — Gasparilla, La Costa, Captiva, Sanibel and Pine — and dozens of smaller keys. This is a great sea shell hunting area, and a few determined "shellers" make a living collecting them and selling to tourists and northern dealers. According to a local legend a shell picked up on the Sanibel beach once fetched twenty-five hundred dollars.

But if your dream is to make a living off your island, your best bet would be to make a resort of it. This is a great place for salt-water game fish, particularly tarpon, and it also attracts more and more plain vacationists every year who just want to lie in the sand and soak up winter sunshine. The big islands in parts are semiurban and have a number of big resort hotels. But the smaller ones offer more privacy and resorts on several of them compete quite successfully with the big ones.

Islands in this neighborhood which already have homes and utilities come rather high. Two reported to me for sale, both with main houses and cottages which would make it easy to turn them into resorts, had asking prices of forty-five and sixty-five thousand dollars respectively. But others more remote and with nothing but small cottages in the way of improvements can be had for small fractions of such prices. And leases of one-acre camp sites on islands owned by the state can be had for fifty dollars or so a season.

A step farther north in the Sarasota and Saint Petersburg area, island properties are mostly in the midst of booming development. Off Sarasota a series of long, narrow keys stretches for thirty miles, but most of them are going through the process of suburbanization. Property values are based on beach frontage and range from twenty to sixty dollars per front foot. Around Saint Petersburg even semisubmerged, mangrove swampy types of islands, which can be made usable only by vast quantities of fill, are quoted at ten to twenty-five thousand dollars.

North and west from Saint Petersburg to the Alabama border, islands are scattered like chips off the Morse code, with tiny dots interspersed among long dashes. With the exception of Santa Rosa Island off Pensacola, none has reached the development stage. Part of Santa Rosa, a seventy-mile strip of magnificent beach, is a National Monument and part a military reservation. The rest is owned by Escambia County, which is attempting to make the island a great recreation center by issuing ninety-nine-year leases at low rentals to commercial developers.

If you have the time for extensive exploring, this stretch of coast is a happy bargain-hunting ground. It is Florida's least exploited region. It is more subject, of course, than the more southerly parts of the state to the phenomenon which Floridians deprecatingly refer to as the cold snap, but it is quite definitely still in the subtropical class.

## *Alabama to Texas*

Few of the islands scattered along the coast of the Gulf of Mexico from Mobile, Alabama, to Brownsville, Texas, are of much interest to would-be escapees. There are several thousand of them, but the great majority are either swamps or waterless sandy deserts. Off Alabama only one, Dauphin Island, is inhabited, and it's a commercial fishing base. Deer Island, off Biloxi, Mississippi, has a few homes. But the few others in the waters off these states are used only by occasional picnickers and campers.

Louisiana has thousands of islands built up out of mud deposited by the Mississippi River. But few of them rise more than a foot or two above high tide, and every storm inundates them completely. Often they are washed away and redeposited further out. Almost the only people who ever set foot on them are the trappers. (Louisiana, oddly, is the foremost state of the nation in production of fur — taking more pelts each year than all of Canada and Alaska put together — chiefly as a result of the efforts of the muskrat trappers among the islands of its coast.)

One of the few habitable islands is Avery Island in Iberia Parish. It's the home of the McIlhenny family and also the source of their income. They make on the island their famous Tabasco Sauce, the red hot essence of the reddest and hottest peppers.

Typical of the dangers of most of the Louisiana islands is the story of Isle Derniere. In the 1840's and 50's it was the

May to October home of New Orleans's wealthiest families, who transported their whole households to the island and lived an elegant, leisurely life far from the city's heat. On August 3, 1856, disaster struck. What seemed at first only an ordinary summer storm suddenly gathered force and began pounding the island to bits with wave after mountainous wave. The whole island was inundated, and more than two hundred of the vacationers were killed. Today, only a few crumbling, jagged ruins of former mansions rise above the sea to mark the spot.

To most people one of the last places in the world to look for islands would be Texas. But its four hundred miles of coast contain several hundred, including a number of considerable interest. The city of Galveston, for instance, is located on the island of the same name but takes up only the northeastern tip of it. The island is thirty miles long, and many fortunate Galvestonians are able to get away to at least semiprivate island homes simply by driving to the far end. Their end of the island is still sufficiently uncluttered to give them bathing, fishing and hunting at their doorsteps.

There are dozens of small islands scattered in bays and lagoons along the Texas coast. A few have been set aside as bird sanctuaries, but many are available for vacation homes. In addition, there are several long, narrow islands with superb beaches, including Padre Island, which stretches for 110 miles from Corpus Christi to Brownsville. They should easily be at least as livable as the similar islands along the coasts of New York and New Jersey.

## Sources of Additional Information

NORTH CAROLINA

United States Coast and Geodetic Survey
Department of Commerce
Washington 25, D. C.
(For charts of the Inland Waterway.)

R. S. Wahab
Ocracoke, North Carolina
(Re Ocracoke Island)

Bill Keziah
Southport, North Carolina
(Re Smith Island)

SOUTH CAROLINA

*Real-Estate Dealers*

D. Trowbridge Elliman
36 Broad Street
Charleston, South Carolina

C. T. Lowndes & Company
12½ Exchange Street
Charleston, South Carolina

William M. Means
60 Broad Street
Charleston, South Carolina

GEORGIA

Brunswick-Glynn County Chamber of Commerce
Brunswick, Georgia

FLORIDA

*General*

For state-owned islands:
Sinclair Wells, Land Agent
State Department of Agriculture
Tallahassee, Florida

For the Florida Keys:

Chamber of Commerce
Key West, Florida

Chamber of Commerce
Marathon, Florida

Upper Keys Chamber of Commerce
Tavernier, Florida

For Santa Rosa Island:

Santa Rosa Island Authority
14 West Government Street
Pensacola, Florida

*Real-Estate Dealers*
Jeffcott Realty Investments
847 First Street
Fort Myers, Florida

J. Otto Kirchheiner
411 Fleming Street
Key West, Florida

Old Island Realty Service
322 Simonton Street
Key West, Florida

W. A. Parrish
P. O. Box 313
Marathon, Florida

Naples Real Estate Exchange
855 Fifth Avenue S.
Naples, Florida

Previews, Inc.
270 S. County Road
Palm Beach, Florida

CHAPTER IX

# Lake Islands of the Mid-continent

THIS CHAPTER covers some six million square miles of ground — all of North America within the coastlines except New England, New York, Quebec and eastern Ontario, which have been covered in previous chapters. In that vast stretch of territory are hundreds of thousands of lakes and thousands upon thousands of islands, but most of them are widely scattered and isolated. Only four states — Ohio, Michigan, Wisconsin and Minnesota — have fairly big concentrations of islands. Manitoba and the northwestern part of Ontario, which I have left to this chapter because it is geographically separate from the rest of the province, also have large numbers. I will cover these states and provinces in detail; of the rest I can give only a few samples which will indicate the kinds of islands you can find if you search long and hard or have a lucky break.

## *Ohio*

Ohio has two quite different types of islands. The Erie Islands, a group of twenty-one which stretch far out into Lake Erie off Sandusky, are much like coastal islands in their nearly complete divorcement from the mainland. The others are scattered among small lakes all over the state and are mostly fairly close inshore.

Five of the largest Erie Islands — Kelleys, Pelee, North Bass, Middle Bass and South Bass, which is also known as Put-in-Bay — have small year-round populations who make their livings chiefly from vineyards and from summer visitors. On the larger islands there are also numerous summer cottages owned by vacationers from Cleveland, Sandusky and other nearby towns. At least one Cleveland businessman who owns a home on Kelleys Island has made an arrangement which most island owners dream of. Every day for five months from late spring to early fall he commutes from the island to his office by plane. The door-to-door trip takes only a little over half an hour.

Homes and homesites on the larger islands vary widely in desirability and in price. Two or three of the smallest, according to local people, seem to be deserted and probably would be buyable if you can run down the owners. One possible contributing reason for their deserted state, though, is the visitation of vicious stable flies which appear in late summer. It takes hard and persistent work to keep them under control.

The most desirable of the small and wholly private islands are in the expensive class. Two which changed hands recently did so at prices rumored to be around $40,000 and $175,000 respectively.

The majority of the islands in the small, interior lakes of

Ohio are in state parks. There are five of these parks with twelve lakes and 135 islands ranging in size from a fraction of an acre to over a hundred acres. Twenty-six are privately owned, and the rest, unlike most such state-owned properties, are not rigidly held open for the use of the whole public. Several of them are open camping grounds, but most are leased to private individuals for long periods.

A fine example of the privately owned island properties is the section of Seminole Island in Indian Lake which belongs to S. F. Hill, the Columbus businessman and island enthusiast whom I mentioned in the first chapter. Seminole is one of a chain of seven islands extending out into the lake in a long arc and connected to each other and the mainland by bridges. That makes it, for purists, "not a real island," but to Mr. Hill and his wife it is heaven.

"It is nearly impossible for me to tell you what the island means to us," he wrote me, "when we go out for the week end after a slam-bang week of hustle and bustle and of being cooped up in an apartment in town. To anyone who likes the outdoors and the water and peace and quiet, I cannot recommend island living too highly."

His section of the island has a curving waterfront. He bought it unimproved and had a small house consisting only of a large living room, bedroom, dinette, kitchen and bath built to his own specifications. The costs make a good guide for other would-be islanders in this area:

| | |
|---|---:|
| Acreage | $ 2,500 |
| House | 7,500 |
| Boat dock | 500 |
| Septic tank | 250 |
| Drilling well | 350 |
| Boat, outboard motor, etc. | 1,000 |
| | $12,100 |

Later, one other expense came up. Because of the way the property curved out into the water and of currents in the lake, the shoreline was slowly eroding. Mr. Hill had a concrete retaining wall built along the water's edge. The cost was $2500. But this is rarely necessary on lake islands.

A few privately owned whole islands in Ohio's small lakes have changed hands recently. Prices ranged from $12,000 to $250,000. Most building sites on the larger islands fall within the $400 to $3600 range.

Ohio also has a number of river islands, chiefly in the Ohio River. Some rise sufficiently high and dry above spring flood levels to make year-round homes. The most interesting of them once was the show place of the Ohio Valley. This is Blennerhassett Island, twelve miles south of Marietta.

The island almost played a role in making the course of our history far different from what it has been. Once owned by George Washington, it was purchased in 1790 by Harman Blennerhassett, a wealthy young Irish immigrant. He spent the then enormous sum of forty thousand dollars on building a palatial mansion and made it the valley's social center.

One of the guests he entertained was the former Vice-President of the country, Aaron Burr, then in disgrace for the killing of Alexander Hamilton in a duel. Burr was in the midst of his fantastic plot to seize a huge chunk of territory in the West and set up a new empire with himself in charge. He decided that the island would make an ideal headquarters and talked young Blennerhassett into joining him. As soon as they began assembling an arsenal, however, news of their plans leaked out, the island was raided, the mansion burned, and both eventually were driven into exile.

## *Michigan*

Michigan consists of two huge peninsulas. The lower peninsula juts north between Lake Michigan and Lake Huron. The Upper Peninsula, as it is formally named, extends eastward from its base on northern Wisconsin between Lake Michigan and Lake Superior. They miss meeting only by the narrow, three-mile margin of the Straits of Mackinac.

Scattered widely over both peninsulas are numerous small lakes, and many of these have small islands. Of far more interest, however, are the hundreds of islands, large and small, along all four shores of the two peninsulas in the three Great Lakes. Nearly all are privately owned summer homes or resorts.

Best known among them is Mackinac Island in the Straits of Mackinac. It has been a famous resort since before the Civil War, when wealthy southern planters began building summer homes along its shores. Now its big claim to fame is its barring of automobiles. The only gasoline-driven vehicle on the island is a fire truck. Bicycles and fringed surreys make a visit there seem like a time-machine trip to the Gay Nineties.

During most of the summer Mackinac teems with tourists. Westward in the middle of Lake Michigan lies a group of eleven islands much farther off the beaten track. They center around big Beaver Island, which is eighteen miles offshore. A ferry service connects the village of St. James on the island with Charlevoix on the lower peninsula.

Some of the smaller islands seem to be of the single-family type, but none of these has been reported to me for sale. On Beaver Island, which is twelve miles long and six wide, and a few of the other large ones, there are many kinds of properties — farms, camp sites, cottages and small-town homes. An airport puts the group within two hours of Chicago.

Back on the other side of the Straits of Mackinac, in Lake

Huron, a group known as Les Cheneaux Islands hugs the shore of the Upper Peninsula. Local boosters like to call them "Michigan's Thousand Islands," but this is far-fetched even for boosterism. There are only thirty-odd, including the tiniest rocky ledges. However, the region does resemble the St. Lawrence River in the crystal clarity of air and water, and in the way many of the islands nestle close together with only narrow channels separating them.

Several quiet old resort hotels are located on the islands, and the shores of most of the larger ones are lined with summer cottages. Many of these are rented by the week. Others can be had for the whole summer. One of the most important claims made for Les Cheneaux, from the point of view of hay fever sufferers, is that they are completely free of ragweed pollen (in fact, this claim is made for the whole Upper Peninsula). Consequently, if you want an island cottage for the August–September ragweed season, it's a good idea to make arrangements well in advance.

Farther east off the tip of the Upper Peninsula and abutting on Ontario's North Channel, the western arm of Georgian Bay, lie dozens of islands ranging from tiny half-acres to Drummond Island, sixteen miles long and twelve wide. The chief concentration is in Potagannissing Bay, but there are several in Munuscong Lake, Lake Nicolet and Lake George. All these bodies of water are part of what is called St. Mary's River, which connects Lake Superior and Lake Huron, and through which passes the United States-Canadian boundary. Some of the smaller islands are owned by the Federal government and are under the jurisdiction of the United States Army Corps of Engineers, which maintains the channel for passage of the iron ore boats from the western end of Lake Superior to the steel mills of the East.

None of the government-owned islands is for sale or rent

or ever is likely to be. (There are a number of similar islands on the Canadian side which were described in Chapter III and which are available under the terms outlined in that chapter.) But the great majority of the American islands are privately owned and occasionally come up for sale or rent under widely varying terms. The three large ones, Drummond, Neebish and Sugar Islands, are partly farmland, and there is extensive lumbering on Drummond. But all three also have large areas devoted only to the summer homes of escapees.

Much closer to the ideal of many escapists, though, are the small islands. "We get our mail about once a week, weather permitting," Mrs. Ann R. Wolcott wrote me (she and her husband own eight-acre Bald Island in Potagannissing Bay off Drummond), "and we are never surprised to have unexpected guests who are surprised that they are unexpected because they sent a telegram, which, of course, hasn't reached us. Quite often, in fact, guests come and go before their telegrams arrive.

"Our island is thickly wooded with white spruce, white cedar, white birch, balsam and one precious Norway pine. We have a few deer, red squirrels, snowshoe rabbits and numerous, although harmless, snakes and spiders. Off our dock we cast for pike, a stone's throw away we catch small-mouth bass, and within sight of the house we fish for perch for breakfast.

"The island gives us perfect respite from the annoyances of city traffic and parking problems, from the frustrations of trying to conduct business clogged with red tape, from the strain of trying to keep up with the Joneses. At first we spent only summers up here (from May to November), but now we are staying for the winter. There is ice fishing and chasing coyotes with ice boats, just to mention a couple of the winter diversions. We pick our Christmas tree from our own private stock, and we don't have colds from living in an overheated house for up here we dress for the out-of-doors all the time.

"With what are we concerned up here? Just two things: what are we having for dinner, and which direction is the wind from."

Another owner of one of these islands was one of the most unusual millionaires ever chronicled — the late Chase Salmon Osborn, onetime governor of Michigan. He assembled a fortune estimated at over fifteen million dollars and gave nearly all of it away to relatives, friends and institutions, keeping only a small annuity for himself to support himself during the last years of his life in quite modest comfort on Duck Island. Osborn liked to claim that he was the only man in the world who regularly shaved in the dark while standing on one foot. Claimed it improved his muscular co-ordination.

He needed a lot of the latter. Until he was past eighty, he lived the rugged life on his island, chopping his own wood, bathing in the bay every morning even in winter and sleeping outdoors on a bed of balsam boughs. One of his guests told a story of watching him row out to capture a bear who was swimming in the bay. Osborn got a line around the animal's neck, but it tried to climb into the boat and almost swamped it. At that point, according to the teller of the tale, Osborn got mad, shoved the bear's head under water and held it there until the animal drowned.

There are a good many other islands scattered along the eastern shore of the lower peninsula in Lake Huron, along the southern shore of the Upper Peninsula in Lake Michigan, and along the northern shore of the Upper Peninsula in Lake Superior. (Except for Isle Royale and the tiny islands surrounding it, which make up Isle Royale National Park, one of the newest and least known of the parks, there are no islands of any consequence far out in the Michigan sections of any of these lakes.) A good many of these inshore islands, such as Williams Island and Wood Island off Munising, are uninhabited and might come quite cheap. There are good highways lining most of the shores of both peninsulas and providing the easiest possible way to go exploring these islands.

## *Wisconsin*

Wisconsin's islands fall into three distinct groups. By far the most numerous are those of the state's seven-thousand-odd inland lakes, concentrated mostly in the north. In addition, there is a group of twenty-six in Lake Michigan and Green Bay off the Door County peninsula, and the twenty Apostle Islands are concentrated in a small area in Lake Superior off Bayfield.

There are at least a couple of thousand inland islands, including those of the Wisconsin, the Chippewa, the Wisconsin side of the Mississippi and other rivers. Brunet Island, about 180 acres in extent, in the Chippewa is one of the few of much size, and it is a state park. A great many are quite small and are used mostly, if at all, as duck hunting blinds in the fall.

Many of the lakes have only one habitable island, which gives the owners of such islands the maximum in privacy. But it also creates a special problem for islanders who want to visit each other, and many are great ones for such visiting. Two University of Chicago professors, for instance, summer on such lonely islands in small lakes about five miles apart west of Green Bay. A friend of mine who spent a summer with one of these families was much amused by the visiting process.

"Almost every evening one family would visit the other. When it was our turn, we climbed in the boat, rowed to shore, drove across to the other lake, then rowed out to the other island, and of course we had to repeat the whole complicated process to get home. They called it the crossing of the land and the waters."

Some six hundred islands in small lakes in the northern part of the state are owned by the state government. Until 1925 they were available for lease to private individuals. In that year the legislature passed an act ending the leasing policy in order to make the islands available for use by more people. The current policy is to restrict them to use by picnickers and fishermen and to prohibit even what the state Conservation Department, which administers them, calls "miscellaneous camping," meaning, presumably, staying on them overnight.

Because there are no large concentrations of these inland islands, either state-owned or private, the only way you can get specific information on any of them is by on-the-spot exploration. Two of the best areas for this are around Rhinelander in the northeastern part of the state and around Spooner in the northwest.

The islands off the Door County peninsula, in Lake Michigan, are grouped together closely. The largest of them, Washington Island, is about five miles square and has twenty-six miles of shoreline. Only 240 miles from Chicago, it is reached by ferry from Gills Rock on the tip of the peninsula, has an airport and a year-round population of over eight hundred. There are several resort hotels on it and numerous summer cottages which can be rented by the week or season.

Some of the twenty-five other islands strewn around the peninsula are too small and rocky and too fragrant with the droppings of gull colonies to be habitable. But at least fifteen or sixteen of them are or have been used as summer homes. One of these, Rock Island off the tip of Washington Island, has a large estate centering around a mansion modeled after an ancient Icelandic feudal hall, but the others are more modest. Two of the smallest, each about nine acres in size, had been unoccupied for several years at last report, and one of them with a cottage may be for sale for about twelve thousand dollars.

Chambers Island, a sandy triangle about three miles on a side which lies five miles out in Green Bay, has a number of properties for sale "at comparatively low prices" according to my informant. Samuel Insull, the Chicago financier, was in the process of trying to make a resort out of Chambers when the law caught up with him and he had to depart hurriedly on his famous voyage to Greece. All that is left of his efforts is a few cottages, now mostly vacant, and a large herd of deer makes up most of the population. There is a lake on Chambers which has a couple of small, uninhabited islands waiting for someone who wants to install himself on a body of land surrounded by water surrounded by a body of land surrounded by water. They'll probably be waiting quite a while. In all my researches I've never encountered anyone who wanted to go that far in shutting out the rest of the world.

Of the twenty Apostle Islands off Bayfield, in Lake Superior, only the largest, Madeline Island, is much used. Madeline has a year-round population of about two hundred dairy farmers and fishermen plus thirty summer homes. Most of the owners of the latter are, oddly, from Lincoln, Nebraska, and the majority of these are third- or fourth-generation descendants of an old-time Lincoln livestock auctioneer, Colonel Woods. The colonel discovered the island back in the late nineteenth century and sold his family and many of his friends on spending summers there.

"On an evening's walk," Robert Ferguson, one of the summerers from Lincoln, told me, "you can see as many as sixty deer, including one pure white albino. Apples and cherries grow wonderfully here, and all our flowers are large and brilliant. We have twenty-six miles of beautiful beaches, but

I must admit that except on hot, still days the water is too cold for anything more than a quick dip."

None of the summer homes on Madeline was reported to me for sale, but I was told that there are building sites available. There seem to be few homes on any of the nineteen other Apostle Islands. Their chief drawback is the near necessity of building a big and expensive dock to protect your boat. When northeasters roar down out of the lake, they can batter to bits anything in their way. The thick winter ice also is rough on anything but a heavy, well-made dock filled with boulders.

## Minnesota

Minnesota, "The Land of Ten Thousand Lakes," has at least as many islands as lakes and probably many more. Some of the larger lakes, such as Vermillion, have hundreds of islands. Thousands of the islands are in the remote wilderness area of the northern part of the state and can be reached only by long boat trips or by a plane equipped with pontoons. Others are within easy reach via the highways.

At one extreme in accessibility and in price was a fifteen-acre section of an island in Lake Minnetonka, just seventeen miles west of Minneapolis, which was offered for sale a couple of years ago. Mostly rolling, wooded land with fine stands of elm, maple and oak, it had a main house of brick with three bedrooms and three baths, a caretaker's cottage, a two-car garage on the mainland opposite, and all conveniences, including telephone. The asking price was fifty thousand dollars.

At the opposite extreme are the camping islands maintained by the United States Forest Service in the Superior National Forest and Chippewa National Forest. Most of these are intended for use by vacationers making one or another of the numerous canoe-and-portage trips laid out through the roadless, lake-dotted flatlands of the Superior National Forest in the northeastern part of the state abutting on the Canadian border. The facilities at these island camps consist only of fireplace, table and latrine, and you must carry with you everything else you need.

In addition, in the Chippewa National Forest summer home-sites are available on Star Island in Cass Lake. You can lease such a site for only twenty dollars a year. At last report fifty-six such sites in three separate groups had been set aside, and ten of them were still unoccupied. Most of the lessees are professional people, and they include families from as far away as California and West Virginia.

To take up such a homesite you have to agree to build only with Forest Service approval of your architectural designs. The policy is to allow only structures which blend into the surroundings, which usually means rough log exteriors. And of course, you can cut only such timber as the Rangers authorize. There's not a single road on the island, but the Forest Service maintains a network of trails.

Besides the Forest Service islands there are also, even within the National Forests, many privately owned island properties. Star Island itself, which is about two miles square, has eleven such privately owned homes and a small resort hotel. Until recently it was possible to reach island properties in or out of the National Forests by plane. But plane traffic was growing by leaps and bounds, and the Forest Service finally had to prohibit flying into the wilderness areas to prevent greedy sportsmen from wiping out every vestige of wildlife. The Federal District Court in Duluth has upheld this prohibition. The decision could be reversed by a higher court, but Congress might then legislate the no-planes rule. So if you hope to be able to fly to and from your island, you had better seek outside the wilderness area boundaries.

There are plenty of islands available outside those boundaries. Big Vermillion Lake, for instance, which is another of those claiming 365 islands and which has eleven hundred miles of shoreline, lies entirely outside the wilderness area. One island there was offered for sale recently by a Hibbing, Minnesota, man. A little over three acres, mostly in virgin timber, it has a large log cabin style main house, a small guest cabin, a boathouse, an icehouse and a workshop. Along with it goes another boathouse and a two-car garage on the mainland half a mile away. The asking price was thirteen thousand dollars.

There are a number of similarly improved islands in Vermillion Lake, in other lakes in this northeastern part of the state and in the lakes around Bemidji to the west. But far more numerous are the unimproved and uninhabited islands. One of the chief concentrations is around Ely, 112 miles northwest of Duluth. There are at least a thousand islands in Burntside, White Iron, Shagawa, Eagles Nest and the dozens of other lakes within a twenty-mile radius of Ely. Probably not more than a hundred of them have summer homes or resorts. A few years ago the Ely Chamber of Commerce, which is extremely island-conscious, gave one island in Burntside Lake to the winner of a radio quiz program. Local authorities say that most of the islands have plenty of timber to spare to provide lumber for building a cabin or cottage. "And," one of them told me, "you can hire expert woodsmen around here who will do most of the building for a ration of liquor, board and room and just a few dollars."

## Manitoba and Northwestern Ontario

Manitoba's three big lakes — Winnipeg, Winnipegosis and Manitoba — all have numerous islands. The provincial government, however, long ago clamped down a strict no-sale policy on those it controls. A few of those acquired by private individuals before this policy was instituted may be for sale, though none was so reported to me.

There are a number of small islands in the lakes around Flin Flon and Cranberry Portage in the west central part of the province and in the Whiteshell Forest Reserve on the Ontario border, and these can be rented on a year-to-year basis. In some cases ten-year leases can be obtained. But the Manitoba government is far less interested in attracting island enthusiasts than is the Ontario government.

For that reason and also because its islands are far more numerous and much easier to reach from most parts of the continent, northwestern Ontario is a better bet. The Ontario part of Lake of the Woods alone (one corner of the lake is in Minnesota) has islands estimated by different authorities as totaling either fourteen or eighteen thousand. Only four thousand have been surveyed, and few even of these have been taken up. Rainy Lake, also shared with Minnesota, has many hundreds, and Lake Nipigon, further east, claims more than two thousand. There are numerous small ones along the northern shore of Lake Superior and countless others in the hundreds of smaller lakes which dot this section of the province.

The great majority are Crown lands available to Canadians and Americans alike under the terms detailed in Chapter Three. To repeat those terms briefly — you can buy islands or parts of islands up to ten acres for forty-five dollars per acre if you intend them for your own private use. You must spend at least five hundred dollars on improvements on the property during the first eighteen months of your tenure. For each acre over five and up to ten you must spend an additional five hundred dollars. If you want to take in paying guests, you can buy up to twenty acres, but you must spend a minimum of two thousand dollars in improvements and, for each acre over ten, an additional two thousand dollars.

As for distances — one of the chief points of entry to this part of Ontario is Fort Frances, which lies across the Rainy River from International Falls, Minnesota. Fort Frances is 320 miles from Minneapolis, which puts it within a couple of days' driving of most parts of the Midwest as far south as St. Louis. Most of the island concentrations, except Lake Nipigon, are within less than a hundred miles of Fort Frances, and most can be reached by good highways. In addition, the Canadian National Railways and the Canadian Pacific Railway cross the area along three different lines, and private planes can be used to reach most of the lakes.

Much of the area is true wilderness, and that is its chief attraction. But it also has island estates in the luxury class for those who want — and can afford — them. One such in Rainy Lake was offered for sale recently. It consisted of two islands connected by a causeway and totaling twenty-two acres. Buildings included an imposing two-story, ten-room mansion built of native stone, a big studio, a guest cottage, a caretaker's cottage, a Finnish bathhouse and assorted others. The asking price was $110,000.

## Other Mid-continent Lakes

As I stated at the beginning of this chapter, lake and river islands are scattered so widely and so thinly through the part of the continent not previously covered that I can give only a few samples. The following is a catchall for what little I have been able to learn of islands scattered in a great arc from Pennsylvania through the South and Midwest on out to the Rocky Mountains.

The director of Pennsylvania's Land Office wrote me: "Please be advised that all the islands in the state were sold by the Penns." In many other parts of the country state governments have retained control of islands and have either made public parks of them or will lease them to vacationers. But the Penns' lack of foresight has not resulted in any great loss to the public. Most of the state's few islands are located in rivers and beset by the spring flood danger.

That danger, of course, doesn't bother true islanders. One family has lived on and farmed a Susquehanna River island for several generations. Nearly every spring there is the possibility of a flood which will completely inundate their home. But they always flatly reject until the last minute the pleas of authorities that they vacate. They have built an overhead basket and pulley connected with a high point on the river shore, but not until the water forces them to the roof of their house do they make use of it to escape.

Southward of Pennsylvania there are only a few individual lake islands in small lakes here and there before you reach the valley of the Tennessee River. There the dams of the Tennessee Valley Authority have created a chain of long, narrow lakes, known as the Great Lakes of the South, which have, according to local authorities, "hundreds of islands." Most lie in Tennessee, but there are a few in the Alabama and Kentucky parts of the development.

They are of all sizes, shapes and conditions. Few have yet been put to any use except by campers. Tennessee state officials say they would like to see some of them developed as resorts for the summer vacationers who are flooding the region in increasing numbers every year. If you are looking for a way of earning a living on an island of your own, this is worth investigating.

Some southern lakes have an interesting though scarcely habitable type of floating island. Orange Lake in northern Florida is half covered by such floaters. They originate when muck gas from the lake bottom floats chunks of mud to the surface. Seeds cling to the mud, put out roots, lace several chunks together and gradually gather more and more of the mud. The process has been going on for so long that some of the islands carry trees thirty feet high and make a fantastic sight as they float majestically around the lake.

Among the Midwest's most interesting islands are those of the Mississippi, Missouri and other large rivers. Some of these are fairly stable and have been brought under cultivation, but in most cases the farmer prudently builds his home on the river's bank. Others are subject to squatters' rights — while they last. Often this is only between one spring flood and the next. Near Muscatine, Iowa, and at a few other points along the Mississippi there are islands with sufficient elevation to be safe against all but the worst floods. Some have been made summer or year-round homes.

Elsewhere in the Midwest and in the Southwest islands are extremely scarce. They are by no means plentiful in the Rocky Mountain states, but there are a number of interest. Utah's Great Salt Lake, for instance, has a dozen. The larger ones are cattle ranches, a purpose for which they are ideal since there is never any loss of strays or to rustlers. And every year the owners get a bonus of new property, for the lake is slowly but quite perceptibly receding. In fact, the process has gone so far that what used to be one of the largest islands became a peninsula a few years ago.

One of the half-dozen islands in Montana's Flathead Lake was advertised for sale recently under the headline "A Rocky Mountain Empire." Four miles long and two wide, it is ringed by a stand of great pines and firs, and most of the interior is rolling grassland rising gently to a ridge a thousand feet above the lake. Herds of deer and mountain sheep roam over it along with about forty Arabian horses offered as part of the deal.

Buildings include three lodges and a dormitory, with room altogether for about fifty guests. The asking price for all this, fully equipped and furnished, was two hundred thousand dollars.

At the opposite financial pole was a recent transaction involving the only island in Idaho's Lake Coeur d'Alene. The shores of the lake have been settled for more than fifty years, but no one ever had paid much attention to the island. A couple of years ago a local citizen decided that he would like to buy it and tried to find the owner. There was none. Turned out that it was part of a parcel of public land which had once been offered for homesteading and had somehow been by-passed and forgotten. He got it simply by filing a home-steader's claim and building a cottage on it.

Nearby Lake Pend Oreille has four quite pleasant little islands. All are privately owned and used as vacation homes. One of them reportedly "might" be for sale, but I could obtain no details on it.

Throughout the Western states, dams built by the Bureau of Reclamation have created huge lakes, and several have a number of islands. It's the policy of the Bureau, however, to keep these for public use, since the recreation attractions created by these lakes have proved a big and unexpected dividend.

The provinces of Alberta and Saskatchewan to the north maintain a similar policy on islands. As one Saskatchewan official told me: "This government is reluctant to sell islands anywhere in the province. The reasons are two. Owners might fence off a beach or playground which the government re-gards as belonging essentially to the people, and owners would have the right to deface the natural beauty of the property."

If you can persuade provincial authorities that you will

commit neither of these atrocities, you might be able to negotiate a deal. Most of their islands, however, are in the far northern reaches of these provinces. Unless the sub-Arctic is the only climate for you, you ought to look around elsewhere first.

## Sources of Additional Information

### OHIO — ERIE ISLANDS

Commerce Club
Kelleys Island, Ohio

Chamber of Commerce
Put-in-Bay, Ohio

### MICHIGAN — LES CHENEAUX ISLANDS

*General*

Les Cheneaux Chamber of Commerce
Cedarville, Michigan

*Real-Estate Dealer*

G. H. Hamel, Realtor
Cedarville, Michigan

### WISCONSIN

Conservation Department
State Office Building
Madison 2, Wisconsin
   (Re state-owned islands.)

Minocqua District Resort Association
Minocqua, Wisconsin

### MINNESOTA

Civic and Commerce Association
Bemidji, Minnesota

United States Forest Service
Duluth 1, Minnesota
  (Re Superior National Forest islands.)

Chamber of Commerce
Box 630
Ely, Minnesota

## MANITOBA

Lands Branch
Department of Mines and Natural Resources
Winnipeg, Manitoba, Canada
  (Rents islands in Manitoba.)

## NORTHWESTERN ONTARIO

Department of Travel and Publicity
Parliament Buildings
Toronto, Ontario, Canada
  (Publications of special interest: "Northwestern Ontario,"
  "Flying Facts About Ontario," and "Waterways to Explore
  — Lake of the Woods.")

Northern Sportsman Magazine
Dryden
Ontario, Canada

Lake of the Woods Tourist Bureau
Kenora
Ontario, Canada
  (For island resorts.)

For further information about individual areas, write to *District
  Forester, Department of Lands and Forests,* at any of the
  following addresses, all in *Ontario, Canada:*

Fort Frances
Geraldton
Kenora
Port Arthur
Sioux Lookout

ALL AREAS IN CHAPTER IX
*Real Estate Dealer*
   Previews, Inc.
   231 South LaSalle Street
   Chicago 4, Illinois

CHAPTER X

# West Coast Islands

GEOLOGICALLY SPEAKING, the North American Pacific coast is an infant several hundred million years younger than the Atlantic coast. As a result, there are far fewer islands off the west coast. The wind and the rain have not had time to carve up the mountains, wash them down into the sea and build long chains of low, sandy islands such as those which stretch from New York to Florida and along the Gulf coast.

Only a few towering submarine mountains raise their heads above the deep waters off the California coast, and except for a few rocks close inshore none make the grade off Oregon. Washington's Puget Sound and the coasts of British Columbia and Alaska are more liberally endowed, partly because their shores don't drop quite so precipitously into such profound oceanic depths as do those further south.

In this chapter I will cover the coastal islands and the few others of interest in the estuaries and inland lakes of the three Pacific coast states, leaving British Columbia and Alaska to the next and final chapter.

## *California*

According to a survey of the state's recreational resources, California has approximately eight thousand lakes covering five acres or more. Most of them perch high in the Sierra Nevada range, and the great majority are near the minimum size. No local authorities would even guess at the number of islands, though there probably are at least a few hundred. But most of the lakes are so remote that they can be reached only by trail. One small island in Lake Arrowhead, owned by the Los Angeles Turf Club, is used for picnicking, but I could find no others being put to any use.

In the delta formed by the junction of the Sacramento and San Joaquin Rivers thirty miles east of the northern arm of San Francisco Bay there is a group of some fifty unusual islands. Until late in the last generation or two, they were vast swamps. Today they are not exactly island paradises, but they constitute some of the nation's richest farmland.

I heard the story of one of the largest of these, Liberty Island, from R. K. Malcolm, head of the company which owns it. Mr. Malcolm and his associates bought in 1917 the seven thousand acres of bulrushes (or, as Californians call them, tules) which then made up the island. They put four floating dredges to work building twenty miles of dikes. crisscrossed the swamp with drainage canals and, as the land slowly dried, plowed under the tules. In all, the making of the island cost several hundred thousand dollars. Yet within eight years of planting the first crops of potatoes and asparagus, the company was able to pay off the entire cost. The alluvial soil is so fabulously rich that the peas, asparagus, lima beans and tomatoes it produces can be shipped profitably across the Rockies to Eastern markets in spite of the high transportation cost.

San Francisco Bay has several small islands. Alcatraz, of course, is the famous Federal penitentiary. Man-made Treasure Island, site of the San Francisco Exposition of 1939–1940, and adjoining Yerba Buena, or Goat Island, are Navy property. Angel Island is one of those which the War Assets Administration offered for sale, but only to public agencies. And Belvedere Island, off Marin County across the Golden Gate from San Francisco, is a residential community.

The Farallon Islands twenty-two miles out in the Pacific off the Golden Gate are barren rocks. Some of them rise a sheer two hundred feet above the sea. They are under the jurisdiction of the United States Coast Guard, and the only inhabitants are the keepers of the lights and their families.

By far the most interesting of California's islands are the Channel Islands strewn along the state's southern coast. They stretch for 155 miles from San Miguel, which lies about forty miles off Santa Barbara, to San Clemente, sixty-five miles off San Diego. Those amounting to more than mere rocks number either nine or eleven, depending on how you count Anacapa, which usually is considered as a single island but actually consists of three separated by narrow channels.

Anacapa and Santa Barbara Islands make up the Channel Islands National Monument. There are no facilities for visitors on either of them, the purpose of creating the monument having been not to attract tourists but "to preserve the unusual geologic, biologic and scientific features." Chief among these are large numbers of fossils, including those of some Pleistocene elephants, and unique varieties of mice, foxes and many other animals and plants which have evolved odd and, to biologists, fascinating differences from their mainland cousins.

Some of the others also are owned by the Federal government. One of these, San Clemente, has a naval air station and at last report was being used mostly for bombing practice targets. Another, San Miguel, is leased to a sheep rancher. Santa Rosa and Santa Cruz are privately owned and devoted mostly to cattle raising and vineyards. It used to be possible to obtain camping and hunting permits from the owners, but trespassers did so much damage that all permits were canceled a few years ago.

Best known of the group, and the only one that takes in visitors, is Santa Catalina. It went through a long series of vicissitudes, including a gold rush that didn't pan out and assorted boom-and-bust real-estate promotions, before being bought in 1919 by the late William Wrigley, the chewing gum magnate. The Wrigley family still maintains on the island a huge cattle ranch and the spring training ground for the Chicago Cubs baseball team which the family owns. But much of the island, which is twenty-two miles long and seven miles across at its widest point, has been leased to operators of various hotels and other tourist attractions.

These last center around the town of Avalon, which has a permanent population of around two thousand and often from two to five thousand visitors per day during its main season from May to September. Accommodations vary from rooms in private homes to luxury hotels, apartments and houses. There's regular ferry service to Wilmington, part of the Los Angeles port twenty-eight miles away, and a regularly scheduled air line. Perhaps the best indication of the decidedly Southern California style of the place is that, when the ferry pulls in from the mainland each day, a set of chimes loudly gives forth with the tune "Avalon."

## Oregon

Along the Oregon coast march miles and miles of clean, white beach bordered by forests of fir and pine which come down to the edge of the sand. In some places the land slopes gently up from the beach. In others great cliffs tower hundreds of feet straight into the air.

An island home off this coast could be one of the most beautiful spots on earth. But there is not a single habitable island anywhere off the whole three hundred miles of it. The only offshore Oregon islands of any kind are rocks habitable only by sea birds or sea lions. Even in the numerous landlocked bays and inlets I could find only one small island. This was in an inlet called Sandlake twenty miles south of Tillamook and was owned by a Tillamook man.

A few of the lakes high in Oregon's Cascade Range have small islands, and I've been told that summer homes have been built on some of them. But they are so few and so scattered that I was unable to obtain details on any of them. As with the other rare few of the Rockies and the Midwest, you would have to make a long search to find them.

The only sizable group of Oregon islands is in the Columbia River, and most of them are downstream from Portland. Formed by silt gathered when the river overflowed its upstream banks during spring freshets and deposited when the current slackened nearer the ocean, they are in their natural state only a little higher and dryer than those of the Sacramento–San Joaquin estuary in California. But like their California counterparts they make fertile farms when diked.

One of the diked islands is the home of Mr. and Mrs. Robert L. Jones. Called Tenas Illihee, a Chinook Indian name meaning "Little Home," it has sixteen hundred acres of diked land. "We run," Mrs. Jones told me, "about a thousand head of Hereford steers, and fattened on grass alone they often have topped the Portland stockyards market and have been given a Grade A rating. I can't get my husband interested in naming any possible price for the island."

There are several other diked islands and hundreds of un-diked ones in the lower Columbia. Many of the latter once were privately owned and have reverted to Clatsop County in default of payment of taxes. Presumably they could be had quite cheaply, but diking is an expensive process. In any case such islands are more in the nature of investments than means of escape.

## Washington

The State of Washington has only a couple of small, rocky islands off its seaward coast. It shares with Oregon some of those in the Columbia River and has a few similar ones in the lower Skagit River north of Seattle. It also has a few isolated islands in inland lakes. But by far the most interesting group in the state — for that matter, in any of the three Pacific coast states — is that of the Puget Sound area. There are about 350 islands altogether, though a good many are too small to be habitable. (For some reason Puget Sound islanders don't go in for claiming 365 islands, "one for each day in the year," as do Easterners who live in island areas. Not one of the dozens of Puget Sound enthusiasts to whom I talked made that claim, although it's much closer to the truth here than in many places where it is made.)

Two Puget Sound counties, Island and San Juan, are com-posed wholly of islands, and there are also a number belong-ing to King County (Seattle) and Pierce County (Tacoma). Many of those in the southern part of the sound near the two cities, of course, are heavily built up. Bainbridge Island, con-nected with Seattle by regular passenger and automobile ferry service, has homes, farms, and a small shipbuilding center. Vashon Island, between Seattle and Tacoma and connected with both by ferry, is similarly near-suburban. But this part of the sound also has a few less built-up islands such as Ketron, a privately owned resort with a deer-hunting preserve only ten miles from Tacoma.

Three of the largest islands of Island County in the northern part of Puget Sound — Camano, Fidalgo and Whidbey — are connected to the mainland by bridges. All have numerous beach and fishing resorts plus large areas of rich farmland specializing in dairy products, berries, and vegetable and flower seeds. Because of the warming influence of the water, spring begins early and the island farmers usually beat their mainland competitors to market with, and get premium prices for, their truck produce. Whidbey (sometimes spelled Whidby) islanders like to describe theirs as "the largest American island immediately adjacent to the United States mainland, save only Long Island, New York," but it can't yet claim to be quite so crowded as its Eastern rival.

Closer to what most island seekers have in mind are those of San Juan County, which lies north of Puget Sound and borders British Columbia. If you count every rock that rises above the water at high tide, the San Juan Islands number 170 or more, but not more than seventy can be considered habitable. These last range in size from an acre or so up to a couple which cover more than fifty square miles.

Most of these islands are beautifully wooded with pine and fir. The view of the Cascade Range and of snow-capped Mount Baker to the east makes newcomers gasp in wonder. Sandy beaches are plentiful, and at low tide they will nearly always yield a fine meal of clams. You can also dig for geoducks (locally pronounced "gooey-ducks"), one of the largest and rarest clamlike shellfish. A single geoduck often makes a meal for two or three people. Dungeness crabs grow nearly as large as Maine lobsters and have a wonderful flavor unlike that of Atlantic coast crabs. The tiny Olympia oysters also have their own unique flavor. And the sound is famous for its Chinook salmon averaging over twenty pounds in weight.

"If heaven's any different from this place," one San Juan islander told me, "I'm not sure I'm interested."

In 1851 the killing of a pig in this paradise almost precipitated a war between the United States and Britain. Five years earlier a treaty had settled the famed "54–40 or Fight" dispute by making the forty-ninth parallel the boundary between Washington and British Columbia. But the region was then little known, and the treaty's language was vague as to exactly where the line should be drawn among the islands. At the insistence of the powerful Hudson's Bay Company, which had long and tight-fistedly ruled the northwest wilderness and which was more than a little disgruntled over the loss of the Washington and Oregon territories, the British government claimed that the treaty had meant to give the San Juan Islands to Britain.

While this dispute was being discussed cautiously on the diplomatic level, several Americans settled on San Juan Island, one of the biggest and most attractive in the archipelago. One day a member of the group found rooting in his carefully tended garden a pig which belonged to a Hudson's Bay Company operative, and promptly shot the porker. The ensuing uproar was long, loud, and full of phrases about national honor. But in the end the diplomats managed to cool off the hotheads by their much maligned but extremely effective method of talking the matter over and postponing decision. Finally, the Emperor Wilhelm I of Germany ("Kaiser Bill's" grandfather) was named to arbitrate the dispute, and in 1872 he awarded the San Juans to the United States.

Eventually, many of the islands went to homesteaders. The last of these were June and Farrar Burn, a couple who probably deserve the title of world's champion island enthusiasts.

June has told the story of some of their island adventures in her charming autobiographical book *Living High* (Duell, Sloan and Pearce — 1941), and she repeated it to me with much gusto and some more recent details.

The Burns married shortly after World War I, settled temporarily in Washington, D. C., and spent all their spare time poring over an atlas in search of the island of their dreams. Chiefly because they liked the shape it had on the map, they chose Puget Sound and wrote the United States Land Office in Seattle announcing that they wanted an island homestead. The answer that there were no more didn't faze them. For several months they kept up a steady stream of gossipy letters to the Seattle office, urging the staff to keep looking for a homesteadable island and outlining their plans for it. Finally they took to the road and arrived some weeks later in Seattle, flat broke but determined as ever.

"Here they are!" the girl at the window shouted happily when they called at the Land Office and gave their names. The whole staff descended on them to shake their hands, slap their backs and promise solemnly that Puget Sound would be ransacked to find an island for them. And it was found — Sentinel Island, small, out of the way, and just what the Burns wanted.

They did several weeks of odd-jobbing to get the money for the boat, tent, bedding, fishing tackle, rifle, tools and staples which they decided were all the equipment they needed. On the day they landed to take possession, such supplies plus fifteen acres of magnificent fir-clad island were all they had in the world.

"But," as June explains, "that was all we wanted. Just an eagle's perch from which we could take a good long look at life."

In the first days they slept on the ground, cooked over an

open fire and lived on fish, seagulls' eggs and seaweed. During the whole first year they had no cash except the few dollars they made selling an occasional fish at a village on a nearby island. But eventually they built a cabin and settled down to raising a family. They spent one year under government contract teaching Eskimos on an isolated Aleutian island, and saved every penny for return to their own island paradise.

Later, when Farrar's veteran's bonus coincided with rock-bottom real-estate prices, they bought twenty-two acres on big Waldron Island, which has a number of homes, and moved there to give their children more companionship. Farrar began making occasional ballad-singing forays to the mainland, and June landed an assignment to cover the San Juans for a Seattle newspaper. But neither likes to spend much time away from their island homes. Lately, however, Farrar has developed a penchant for bronchitis, and he and June are considering selling or swapping Sentinel Island for one to the south as sunny and warm for the winter as Sentinel is sunny and cool for the summer.

"As a matter of fact," June told me, "empty islands look to me so sort of pioneery and jolly that they make me home-sick. Farrar and I would like to begin again at the beginning, now that our sons are grown up and on their own."

Waldron's fame as a peaceful, quiet haven has spread throughout the Puget Sound area. A few years ago the inhabitants decided to hire a combination postmaster and school-teacher. They had only to pass the news of their quest for such a man by word of mouth. In response they were almost swamped by applicants who arrived posthaste in every conceivable kind of boat.

It was at about this time that eight young couples, most of them just out of college, settled on Waldron and vehemently declared their permanent independence. They have made the declaration stick, too, with remarkable perseverance and ingenuity. Nearly all of them have built their own houses, using timber, stone and other materials available on the island and no labor other than their own and help from each other in the form of old-fashioned, neighborly building "bees." Each has worked out his own design, and some of the results are extraordinarily attractive homes.

All have found ways of earning what little money they need without compromising their independence. One young chemical engineer, for instance, spends one week each month working in a laboratory. Some spend two or three months each summer working in Alaskan fishing boats and canneries. Others work in the Yakima and Wenatchee apple harvests. And one couple, John and Gudrun Goodrich, have made their home a small summer resort.

An irregular "sky-ferry" service, operated by a Bellingham airplane pilot, is Waldron's chief connection with the outside world. The pilot good-naturedly does much of the shopping for the islanders so that many of them go for months without visiting the mainland. A small boat brings mail three times a week but no passengers. When anyone needs something too big for the plane or mailboat, the islanders go in together to hire a bigger boat.

But Waldron is by no means the only private or semiprivate paradise among the San Juan Islands. Many of the smaller ones are owned by single families who can, when they wish, shut out the rest of the world even more completely than does Waldron. One of these is the summer home of a University of Washington professor and his family.

During World War II the professor and his two sons were scattered around the globe on Army assignments. Before the war they had spent summers on one of the larger San Juan islands and had dreamed idly of owning a small one of their own someday. Army life made the dream more vivid. When someone wrote the professor and remarked in a by-the-way that one of the islands was for sale, he called a family conference by mail. The decision was never in doubt, though it took hard scrabbling to round up the money.

After the war the thirty-odd acres of woodland and beach were all theirs. They have done most of the clearing and building themselves and have even managed to beachcomb much of the lumber for their house in the form of weathered logs washed up on their shores. The result is a wonderfully comfortable and appealing little island kingdom.

Some years ago another small island housed for a while a religious colony whose fate still puzzles the natives. The group appeared from out of nowhere one day, took over the island and cut itself off from outsiders except for occasionally and noncommittally ordering groceries. A year or so later the group departed just as suddenly and mysteriously as it had arrived, and it hasn't been heard of since.

On the larger islands, of course, you can't cut yourself off from the world so completely. But if you don't insist on absolute privacy, they do have advantages. The two biggest are Orcas, which covers fifty-seven square miles, and San Juan, a little over fifty-five square miles. (Waldron, which covers four and a half square miles, is sixth in area.)

Nearly all the big ones have regular connections with the mainland by plane and/or ferry, including automobile ferry. Some have telephone service, city-style water supplies and sewer systems, and good roads. But none is so populous and built up that it isn't possible to find a corner where you can get off by yourself and use these civilized conveniences only if and when you feel like doing so.

Orcas is almost cut into three separate islands by two deep indentations called East Sound and West Sound, and it has numerous other private little bays and inlets. Part of it is set aside as Morgan State Park, in the midst of which Mount Constitution towers twenty-four hundred feet above the surrounding sea. A good highway runs to the summit, from which there is an unusual 360-degree view out over hundreds of miles of island-dotted waters, with Mount Baker, Mount Rainier and the Olympics in the background. You can also see British Columbia's Vancouver Island — to the southwest. (It's nearly always a surprise to newcomers that most of the San Juans lie well to the north of the southern tip of this huge Canadian island.)

There are numerous small resort hotels and cottages for rent around the villages of Orcas, East Sound, West Sound, Deer Harbor, Olga and Doe Bay on the island. Widely diversified farms make it almost completely self-sustaining in food. And it even has a couple of inland lakes to provide freshwater fishing if you get tired of hauling huge salmon out of the surrounding straits.

San Juan Island has the county seat and metropolis, Friday Harbor, a village of around a thousand population. Its area is half lush green woods and farms, half hilly treeless rangeland used mostly for cattle and sheep ranching. It, too, has resorts and rentable cottages, though fewer than Orcas.

Several of the other large San Juans, such as Lopez and Decatur, have small hotels or, more often, groups of cottages and cabins. None of these is of the type of which you can expect, or which will expect of you, anything in the way of swank. You can find modern accommodations with all the conveniences, if that's what you want. But if you want a place far off in some corner of an island with maximum privacy, you may have to make do with rudimentary plumbing and kerosene lamps.

There usually are a few small islands and properties on

larger islands for sale in the San Juans, but they don't come cheap. As I remarked in the first chapter, the islands were "discovered" in a big way during and after World War II, and property values have zoomed. Many such values doubled, redoubled and re-redoubled during the '40's.

One whole island of about two hundred acres with two cottages, long stretches of beach and a fine stand of timber was being offered a couple of years ago for twenty thousand dollars. Another of about the same size and character with a mansionlike house was quoted at "around" fifty thousand. The only ones reported to me at under ten thousand dollars' asking prices were under ten acres and unimproved.

Among properties with homes on the larger islands, one with nearly a mile of waterfront was quoted at twelve thousand dollars. Another, extended across the neck of an island, has five hundred feet of beach on each end and an asking price of ten thousand dollars. A third, with sixteen hundred feet of sandy beach and a house offered furnished, was advertised at eleven thousand five hundred.

The only thing in the way of a great bargain of which I have heard was an odd transaction reported in a Seattle newspaper. It seems that a Seattle citizen had won a three-acre San Juan island in an essay contest but had decided he didn't want it because he was in the midst of building a mainland house. He did need a car, though, and in return for one he traded the island to a woman.

A reporter called on the lady to learn her plans for the island. Why, he asked, had she made the trade?

"I just wanted to own an island," was her answer. And she stuck to that story through thick and thin.

Did she plan to build a house on it? the reporter persisted. She didn't. Had she ever seen it? She hadn't. Only pictures. Was there any romantic history attached to the place? Not that she knew of. Had she ever heard of buried treasure on it? No.

"It's just," she firmly concluded the interview, "that I've always wanted to own an island."

One drawback common among salt-water islands does not apply on many of the San Juans. Nearly all the large and most of the small islands have plenty of fresh water. In fact, on calm days fishermen who know just where to dip their buckets can find fresh water even at certain spots out in the sound. It seems that there is an artesian flow boiling up from the bottom of one of the channels. On some of the islands the subterranean fresh water is under such pressure that well drills occasionally produce small geysers.

You can reach the San Juans via plane — from Seattle, about seventy miles away, to Orcas Island. But if you want to explore, you can get a closer look on the trip via automobile ferry from Anacortes or passenger ferry from Bellingham. The latter makes a day-long round trip winding among the islands and stopping at several to load and unload cargo. You can also, of course, rent a motor or sailboat at either town, but there are places in the channels among the islands which require expert seamanship in the negotiating.

If you take the time to get acquainted, you will find some remarkable characters among the islanders. Many families have lived in the islands for two or three generations and would never dream of moving to the mainland, where, as one old-timer put it, "you're always a-bunting into someone."

Perhaps the best indication of the spirit of the San Juans is a local invention they call a wickiup. It consists of a long bench built on the beach from driftwood gathered there. A shingled roof shades it, and racks at both ends hold books and magazines. There's a place for a beach fire in front, and a cupboard along the back holds food and drink. The foot-rest in front of the bench is a log set on the bias so that short legs can reach it at one end and long legs at the other.

## Sources of Additional Information

CALIFORNIA

Chamber of Commerce
Avalon, California
  (Re Santa Catalina Island.)

Superintendent
Sequoia & Kings Canyon National Parks
Three Kings, California
  (Re Channel Islands National Monument)

Division of Information
National Park Service
Department of the Interior
Washington 25, D. C.
  (Re Channel Islands National Monument.)

WASHINGTON

*General*

Camano Island:
Stanwood Commercial Club
Stanwood, Washington

San Juan Islands:
Chamber of Commerce
Bellingham, Washington

Lopez Island Commercial Club
Lopez, Washington

*Real-Estate Dealers*

San Juan Islands:
C. K. McMillin
National Bank of Commerce Building
Bellingham, Washington

H. F. Furrow
Sound View Real Estate & Insurance Company
East Sound, Washington

William A. Eastman & Company
410 Green Building
Seattle, Washington

V. F. Pavey
322 15th Ave. N.
Seattle, Washington

CHAPTER XI

## Coastal Islands of British Columbia and Alaska

For most people to whom I have spoken, the first reaction to the name "Alaska" is "frozen north." The comparatively few Americans who have any reaction at all to the name "British Columbia" tend to place it in the same category. Many, however, then pause and say something like, "Oh, but there's some sort of gulf stream or something, isn't there?"

Both reactions are quite correct. Much of Alaska and a large part of British Columbia have extremely frigid winters. But their coasts are warmed by the Japanese Current and have equable climates. Juneau, Alaska, for instance, has an average January temperature of 29° and a July average of 55°, though on rare occasions the thermometer has sunk as low as 21° below zero and has risen as high as 89° above.

Both coasts are well endowed with islands. I'll start with those of the Canadian province. In general, they are the more accessible and the more readily available to would-be Crusoes.

## British Columbia

The province of British Columbia covers 366,000 square miles, which makes it nearly half again the size of Texas. Until World War II it was for the most part a vast, quiet backwater, partly primitive wilderness and partly super-genteel, "more British than Britain." In the last decade a still rapidly accelerating growth in population and industry has gotten under way, based chiefly on the harnessing of the almost limitless water power of the coastal rivers.

But this has not in the least disturbed the peace and quiet of the islands. Scattered from a point just across the international line from Washington State's San Juan group to the Alaskan border, the British Columbia islands offer the best and the most chances to escape to an island on the continent's west coast. As usual, they haven't been counted, and the best estimates I could get were that they number, according to one provincial authority, "hundreds," or, according to another, "thousands." Judging from large-scale maps, it seems certain that there are at least two thousand and perhaps many more.

There are a few in the mountain lakes of the interior, but these are mostly too inaccessible to be of interest. By far the most intriguing are those in the straits between big Vancouver Island's east coast and the mainland. But there are hundreds of others along the west coast of the big island and off the mainland to the north which would appeal to anyone seeking to make his escape complete by cutting off all but the most attenuated contacts with the outside world.

The southern tip of Vancouver Island lies just across the Strait of Juan de Fuca from the northern tip of Washington's Olympic Peninsula and about seventy miles northwest of Seattle. From that point the island stretches northwest for

282 miles and covers altogether some thirteen thousand square miles, nearly half the area of Ireland. Its distance off the mainland varies from a maximum of forty miles in the south to as little as two miles near its northern end.

Victoria, the province's capital, lies at the southern end of the big island and nearly always impresses new arrivals as the unlikeliest city imaginable. It seems to belong not at this remote end of the earth but in some quiet shire of olde England. That's exactly the impression it seeks to give not only to visitors but also to its own inhabitants. Large numbers of the latter are retired members of the British colonial civil service who gravitate thither from all over the world. They yearn back to the days when a gentleman automatically dressed for dinner even in the jungle, and that is the tone they have set for Victoria.

Many of the small islands off Victoria and northward to Vancouver, the province's chief city, which lies on the mainland some fifty miles almost due north of Victoria, have been taken up by such retired Britons. Cruising in the area you pass lovely little islands which are all green lawn and clipped hedges, much like Devonshire manors except that instead of stables or garages they have docks and breakwaters. Other islands are farms or ranches. Still others are the summer homes of Americans who recently have been flocking to British Columbia in larger and larger numbers, chiefly from California.

Locally, the Victoria–Vancouver group is known as "the gulf islands," though none of the waters in the area is named the gulf of anything. (They are either straits, sounds, bays, channels, inlets or coves.) Nearly all these islands now are privately owned. Others to the north are Crown lands and can be purchased from the provincial government at prices even lower than those offered by the Province of Ontario.

But since the so-called gulf islands are more accessible and since there are usually many properties among them for sale at a wide range of prices, I will take them up first.

On bright days many of the islands are almost dazzling to look at because of the richness and intense greenery of their foliage set against the white sand beaches. Most have good growths of fir, cedar, balsam and hemlock plus a few maples, oaks and alders. Wild flowers, particularly violets, lilies and evergreen arbutus, grow densely along the shores of some. There are few towns of any size even on the larger ones but many small hamlets including a school, church, general store and post office.

One fairly typical islander is a retired Canadian who owns a small, isolated section of one of the large islands. His teen-age son goes to school on the mainland and spends only week ends on the island. But the parents spend all their time there except for occasional visits to Vancouver "just to make ourselves," as the father puts it, "more satisfied to stay here." With a small kitchen garden, a few chickens, an excellent oyster bed and almost unlimited fish and game, they can go for weeks at a time without grocery deliveries.

Not so typical is the story of Mr. and Mrs. David Conover and Wallace Island. Conover, a Californian, had spent several summers as counselor at a boys' camp on the island in the late '30's. After Pearl Harbor the camp folded, and Conover went into the air force, saw action in the Pacific, and spent many hours dreaming of the island. In 1946, after his discharge, he took his wife to British Columbia and visited Wallace.

"We romped all over the island like school kids," he told me. "She liked it as much as I did. I had never imagined anyone would part with it, but when we accidentally discovered that it was for sale for $17,500, we headed straight back to

Los Angeles, sold our property there and raised the money."

Late that summer the Conovers re-entered Canada as settlers (but keeping their United States citizenship) and became proprieters of an island all their own. About three miles long and covering 250 acres, Wallace lies almost exactly halfway between Victoria and Vancouver and has an excellent natural harbor shaped much like San Francisco Bay. When they arrived, it had an old caretaker's shack, several tumbledown buildings from the old camp, a good spring — and that was all.

"Just how we weathered that first winter," he told me, "I don't quite know. We stayed in the shack and spent the days building our house and the nights studying books about how to build a house. I don't think I ever had touched a hammer before, and I'm sure there are few people who know less about the country way of life than we did. But eventually I mastered carpentry, plumbing and the rudiments of several other trades, and we built ourselves a very comfortable house."

Remarkable accomplishment though this is, it's barely the half of what the Conovers have done. Their purpose was to make not only a home but also a living out of their island by taking in paying guests during part of the year. In six years, mostly with their own hands, they have built several completely modern and remarkably attractive cottages of native cedar with knotty pine paneling inside, kitchenettes, baths, and complete seclusion at different spots around the island. The result is one of British Columbia's most highly rated (by the provincial government) small resorts. By 1951 it had become so successful that Conover was able to add to his domain the two lovely Secretary Islands. They lie just off Wallace and are about the same size. Income from the sale of a bit of Wallace Island timber, just when lumber prices hit a peak, helped make the addition possible.

Actually, the Conovers almost could get by without income from guests. Their large garden and small apple orchard produce in quantity. They get eggs and fryers from their flock of chickens and lambs from a small herd of sheep. From April to October salmon up to a hundred pounds in weight are always available offshore and can be canned and frozen in large quantities for winter use. Conover "farms" the oyster beds in his cove, and the oysters are edible the year round no matter what letter the name of the month may lack. During the summer months big Dungeness crabs also frequent the harbor.

Ducks are in season and plentiful from mid-October to January, and black Bryant and snow geese from mid-December to March. Even quail, pheasant, blue grouse and ruffed grouse occasionally turn up in the fall. There are also a number of deer on the island, but they are far too tame for hunting. In fact, they are even tamer than the sheep, which have run wild.

Mink do well on the island, and Conover is gradually increasing their numbers by trapping female mink on nearby uninhabited islands and releasing them on Wallace. Already he can harvest a dozen or more pelts every winter and still keep increasing his stock. He mails them to New York, and even when the market has been bad they have brought nearly thirty dollars apiece.

Some of Conover's experiences in learning the ropes of island life have been on the hectic side. It was in the first year that he decided to raise sheep. The man from whom he bought them on the mainland told him that the best way to get them over to the island in his small boat was to tie their feet and make them lie down in the boat's bottom.

"It wasn't until I was halfway across," Conover reminisces, "that I realized they were double-jointed. By that time they had wiggled loose. I couldn't leave the tiller, and for a while the question seemed to be whether they would trample me to death or swamp the boat first. They finally jumped overboard and swam to the island. I can assure you they are here to stay."

Another time he bought a tractor and hired a scow on which to float it across from the mainland. With help he beached the scow, drove the tractor onto it and floated it off the beach at high tide. Then the scow started to leak. Conover bailed madly and urged the boatman he had hired to tow the scow to put on speed. Halfway across a squall came up.

"I didn't know whether to try to keep the tractor from sliding off and let the scow slowly sink under it or to keep working on the leak and just pray the tractor would stay in place. Before I stepped ashore on Wallace, I think I aged ten years. But we did manage to get the tractor across."

Then there was the water problem. At first the spring, which produces several hundred gallons a day, was more than enough, but another source had to be found to supply the guest cottages. Conover found a well-driller in Victoria who agreed to bring over his truck and drilling rig in a landing barge. But to get the truck from the beach at Wallace inland to the area where Conover wanted to drill, a road was needed. Conover built it himself with pick and shovel, spending several long weeks on the job.

The driller arrived on schedule with his rig, picked his spot and started down — at a charge of ten dollars per foot. At a depth of 220 feet there was no sign of water. Conover bought a "diviner" and picked another spot. At sixty feet the drill struck coal. At eighty-five feet it was still boring through coal and was hauled back up. This time Conover bought a textbook on geology and picked the third spot on the basis of what he learned from it. Science triumphed over superstition when a two-thousand-gallon-per-day well came in at twenty-five feet.

In spite of this long, harrowing and expensive experience, Conover thinks water should be a less important consideration in choosing an island than a good harbor.

"If worse comes to worst," he told me, "you can always haul in water. I know islanders who do it regularly. But without shelter for your boat and a good site for a dock, which also needs protection, you are bound to be in trouble a lot of the time. I've watched one of my neighbors, a wealthy Californian, move his yacht from one side of his island to the other several times in a single day just to try to shelter it from strong, changing winds. He had no cove of any kind. So now he has spent fifteen thousand dollars for a breakwater, and he's still in trouble because the boat goes aground behind it at low tide."

A few years ago one of the Conovers' first guests, another Californian, became so enamored of the island that he wanted to buy one for himself. He made a few inquiries and discovered one nearby which was for sale. It covers twenty-seven acres, is heavily wooded, has a fine harbor and a flowing spring, but had no improvements. He got it for thirty-eight hundred dollars.

Even at that time this was a bargain, and prices have been climbing steadily since then. A more recent offering in the gulf islands group was a seven-acre island, also wooded and with a fair harbor. The only improvement was a small cabin, and the asking price was sixty-five hundred dollars.

A more elaborate type was an eighty-acre island with a three-bedroom house. It had, in addition, a one-room guest cottage and a two-room caretaker's house. Utilities included electricity, a good well with a pump and modern plumbing in all the buildings. The asking price was fourteen thousand dollars.

One Vancouver real-estate firm which lists numerous island properties gave me a set of nine examples. It is likely that most of these will have been sold by the time you read this, but they will give you a good idea of the range of island types and prices.

1. A fifty-acre island sixteen miles from Vancouver. There are six cottages and a boathouse and four wells from which water is piped to a four-thousand-gallon storage tank. Price: $25,000.

2. 247 acres about a mile from #1. This has eight cottages and ample water supply for all of them. It also has four good harbors. Price: $50,000.

3. About fifty miles northwest of Vancouver is a group of four offered together or separately. The first of these has 186 acres of good soil but no improvements whatever. Price: $6000.

4. The second of this group is 540 acres and has a few old farm buildings. Originally, it was put into orchard. The anchorage is good. Price: $16,000.

5. The third has 175 acres and good timber but no improvements of any kind. Price: $5000.

6. The fourth has 234 acres and was used for a number of years as the summer home of its California owner. Some time ago the house burned down, and it was never replaced. There's a good well and a small stand of timber. Price: $7500.

7. Another similar ex-summer home, the house on which also was destroyed by fire, lies two miles off the mainland thirty-two miles northwest of Vancouver. It covers fifty-one acres. Price: $7500.

8. Just off Vancouver Island and thirty miles west of Vancouver (city), two islands covering 207 acres altogether and joined by a reef at low tide offer a neat

way of keeping warring factions of your family apart for most of the day. Six acres of one of the islands has been put under cultivation and consists mostly of an orchard with several kinds of fruit. The anchorage and water supply are both excellent. Price: $25,000.

9. A group of two large islands and two small islets about a hundred miles northwest of Vancouver are offered only together. The islets cover about two and a half acres and lie just off the more northerly big island. One has timber, but the other is bare. There's no known water on either.

The big north island has 237 acres, half of which is rock rising to a height of 420 feet and with only scrub growths of jack pine and fir. Down the center runs a valley well timbered with fir and heavy cedar, and the soil is rich black loam. No timber ever has been cut, and former owners used it chiefly as a game preserve. It is well stocked with deer, grouse and other game.

The south island has 457 acres, and its central valley has been logged and cleared. The house is located here (unfortunately, I have no description of it), and there is an acre of garden fenced against the deer and planted. Three reservoirs on a hillside assure the water supply, which is fed to the house by a gravity system. From thirty to forty acres of the land could be cleared and would make good cropland. There are four small bays with anchorage and beaches on the south and east sides of the island, and the rest of the shoreline is mostly rock. About two million board feet of timber could be harvested plus perhaps two thousand cedar telephone poles and pilings.

The asking price for all this was $125,000.

All the above, of course, are for those who want an island all to themselves. Properties on the larger islands range a good deal lower in price. Texada Island (104 square miles), Salt

Spring (69 square miles), Galiano (21 square miles) and the dozen others of similar size have both small communities and isolated coves. In the latter you can achieve nearly as much privacy as on a completely separate island.

Most of the people on the larger islands are much like those who own the small ones. There usually are a number who spend only summers at the island. Year-round residents include a good many retired or semiretired Canadians, Britishers and Americans. The rest make their livings operating resorts or by a combination of farming, commercial fishing and logging.

One property on Galiano Island offered for sale not long ago comprises fifty acres and has thirteen hundred feet of water frontage. It also has what was described as "a good barn and a house of nominal value." There are fruit trees, a creek running through the property and a good well. The asking price was only twenty-five hundred dollars. I'm told, however, that this is unusually low and that frontage on this and other large islands is rapidly rising in price.

Many of the most desirable small gulf islands are located close along the shores of or between two neighboring large islands. Wallace Island, for instance, is between Salt Spring and Galiano. This provides some degree of shelter from the roughest weather and usually makes it possible to reach the small island in the smallest of outboard motorboats by staying in the lee of the big island.

One such sheltered island, between Texada and Lasquite, was reported to me for sale some time ago, and I haven't heard that it has yet changed hands. It covers 234 acres, has two wells and a good harbor, and its virgin timber includes many huge firs as much as twelve feet in circumference. The owner, a Los Angeles man, bought it in the early '20's, built a rugged lodge and spent summers there with his family for many years.

But since the crash of 1929 he has been able to return only at rare intervals, and the lodge has fallen into disrepair and the clearing has become overgrown. He told me he would sell for ten thousand dollars or would trade for property in or around Los Angeles.

For great island bargains you must go north to the straits between the mainland and the northern end of Vancouver Island and to the open coast of British Columbia beyond. It is a coast deeply and steeply indented by great fjords cut through the sea cliffs by rivers pouring down from the continental divide, only two to three hundred miles inland. Norwegian visitors have been known to admit that it compares favorably in scenery with the spectacular coast of their country.

Although much of the province's postwar industrial and population growth has been in this region, it still is sparsely settled, frontier country. No highways skirt the coast, and except for a long lonely spur of the Canadian National Railways to Prince Rupert near the Alaska border, the only ways you can penetrate the area are by plane or boat. The famous Inside Passage, so called because it winds between the islands and the mainland, is the chief steamer route to Alaska.

Among the features of an Inside Passage trip are the schools of "small" whales, sometimes called blackfish. They are said to be small because they seldom grow over thirty-six feet in length. This may not be much for a whale, but when a group of such junior leviathans gets to diving, surfacing and generally helling around near your boat, you are not likely to feel disappointed by their lack of maximum bulk.

Islands here range up to several hundred square miles in size, and most of the good farmland on the bigger ones has been taken up. Much of the territory is so rocky and hilly that there is not enough fertile soil in any one spot to support a family. Often, the settlers have to eke out their farming with fishing, logging and fur trapping.

But the prices on those islands which still remain Crown lands, as many of them do, are rock bottom. In fact, if you are a Canadian or if you will declare, and follow through on, your intention to become a Canadian citizen, you can get some of them for nothing. This is by a process called pre-empting. You can, however, pre-empt land only for agricultural purposes, and as I've already said, there's not much good farmland left among the islands.

If you want to look further into this, the Superintendent of Lands in Victoria will give you details. (You will find at the end of the chapter his full address and a list of the pertinent publications he can send you.) Briefly, what you have to do is find land still owned by the Crown and not reserved for some special purpose, and convince the proper authority that it is arable. You must then spend at least ten months a year for five years living on it and bringing part of it under cultivation. At the end of that time it's all yours. There are, of course, various other requirements and exceptions too complicated to go into here, but these are the basic details.

Somewhat simpler is the process of purchasing Crown lands. And, unlike pre-empting, this can be done by Americans who don't want to become Canadian citizens. The minimum price on islands or parts of islands is ten dollars per acre, but the Superintendent of Lands can set a higher price if he wishes. The most you can buy is 640 acres, and you are supposed to take at least forty acres or four hundred dollars' worth. In the case of islands under forty acres in area, this last provision can be waived.

So far as the law is concerned, you can buy an island sight unseen through an agent if you want to go about the business in that odd fashion. If the land hasn't been surveyed, you

must pay for this, and you must make a deposit of fifty cents
per acre when you submit your application. If the authorities
decide that it isn't in the public interest to sell the island,
or if you decide to back out before the deal is completed,
the deposit is refunded minus a few minor fees. You may be
required to make improvements amounting in value to not
less than five dollars per acre within four years, but this requirement is not so systematized as in the case of Ontario
Crown lands.

There are few, if any, such Crown lands left on islands
along the more accessible, southern parts of the British Columbia coast. But if you want to get far, far away from it
all and if you feel capable of coping with a wilderness, the
islands to the north will neatly fill your bill. The Queen
Charlotte Islands, for instance, lie fifty miles offshore and are
separated from the mainland by Hecate Strait, the name of
which is indicative of its temperament. The name of one of
the hundred and fifty islands in the group also is highly appropriate: "All Alone."

## *Alaska*

There are tens of thousands of islands in the Gulf of Alaska,
along the Aleutian chain and northward. But as veterans of
the World War II Aleutian campaign can and, at the drop
of a hat, will testify, "habitable" is not the word for any but
a rare few of them, and you easily can get an argument about
those. Many are rocky crags, and the weather consists chiefly
of alternate fog and rain.

More to the point is the Alexander Archipelago, the group
of several hundred islands which stretches south from Juneau
like drops from a melting icicle. Nearly all of these are in
the Tongass National Forest and under the jurisdiction of the

United States Forest Service. Although four of the territory's chief towns — Ketchikan, Wrangell, Petersburg and Sitka — are scattered among the islands, most are untouched by civilization.

Their chief drawback is the inordinate amount of rain that pours down upon them in some places more than three hundred days out of the year. The Japanese Current, which keeps them warm, also brings moist air which begins wringing itself out as soon as it reaches the outer islands. Along much of the British Columbia coast the seaward sides of the big islands, such as Vancouver Island, have mountains which trap some of the rain and keep the inner islands reasonably dry. But more gets through the Alexander Archipelago, and Ketchican is drenched by 150 inches — 12½ *feet* — of rain per year. Juneau has eighty-odd inches of it and most of the rest of the area at least that much.

If you can stand the dampness, though, it produces some fine results in the way of wild berries. Cranberries, huckleberries, red and black currants, salmonberries, thimbleberries and strawberries grow thickly. Goose tongue and wild parsley make fine greens, and wild rice, a costly luxury in the States, is plentiful. Fish, shellfish and game are, of course, inexhaustible.

The Forest Service offers two different types of propositions on island properties in the Tongass National Forest. You can buy a homesite of up to five acres for only $2.50 an acre. Such homesites, however, are not made available in parts of the archipelago far from established communities. Isolated tracts sold in the past usually have been abandoned sooner or later because the buyers got lonesome.

Alternatively, you can lease a whole island or even a group of islands up to a total of a thousand acres in area. The charge is $12.50 per year for up to five hundred acres and twenty-five dollars per year for 501 to one thousand acres. In theory, the islands can be leased for any purpose of which the Forest Service approves. But in practice most such leased islands are used as fur farms. This is no business for an amateur, though, and unless you can prove that you know what you are up to you are likely to encounter a friendly but firmly discouraging attitude.

# Sources of Additional Information

BRITISH COLUMBIA

*General*

Superintendent of Lands
Department of Lands and Forests
Parliament Buildings
Victoria, British Columbia, Canada
(Some publications are: "How to Pre-empt Land," "Some Questions and Answers Regarding British Columbia," "Crown Lands — Purchase and Lease," "Vancouver Island," "Queen Charlotte Islands.")

Government Travel Bureau
Department of Trade and Industry
Victoria, British Columbia, Canada
(Some publications are: "British Columbia, Canada," "Vancouver Island Guide," "Auto Courts and Stopping Places," "Hunting and Fishing in British Columbia.")

Comox Agricultural and Industrial Association
Courtenay
British Columbia, Canada
(Re Gulf Islands.)

*Real-Estate Dealers*

P. Leo Anderton and Company
Courtenay
British Columbia, Canada

Comox Valley Lands
Courtenay
British Columbia, Canada

Frederick Field Agencies
Courtenay
British Columbia, Canada

Salt Springs Land, Ltd.
Box 35
Ganges, British Columbia, Canada

Prince Rupert Realty Company
435 Third Avenue W.
Prince Rupert, British Columbia, Canada

G. Percy Tinker & Company
Box 508
Prince Rupert, British Columbia, Canada

Craddock and Company
805 Vancouver Block
Vancouver, British Columbia, Canada

Pemberton Realty Corp., Ltd.
418 Howe Street
Vancouver, British Columbia, Canada

H. A. Roberts, Ltd.
530 Burrard Street
Vancouver, British Columbia, Canada

## ALASKA

Regional Forester
United States Forest Service
Box 1631
Juneau, Alaska

Experimental Fur Station
Petersburg, Alaska
   (Re fur farming.)

# Naming Your Island

THOUGH it often is considered rather affected to give a name to a mainland home or estate, an island needs a name for navigational and postal delivery purposes, if none other. The great majority, indeed, already have names. It frequently happens, though, that the purchaser of an island doesn't like its name and wants to change it. This can be done in some cases, but it isn't easy.

Among your family and friends, of course, you can call your island whatever you please. But to change it officially and on the maps — or, in the rare case of an unnamed island, to make a name stick — you need the co-operation of the Division of Geography of the United States Department of the Interior (in Canada the Geographic Bureau has a similar function).

The division is the United States government's final authority on all place names used on government maps, and one of its chief purposes is to prevent the confusion which results from arbitrary and unnecessary changes in names. If your island has an old, well-established name which is generally accepted by the other inhabitants of the area, you won't get much co-operation in changing the name. In fact, attempts to make arbitrary changes in name are the bane of the division's staff members' professional lives.

You will get co-operation, however, if the old name falls into any of these three categories:

1. A too common name, such as Long Island or Round Island, is, from the division's point of view, worse than none. There are hundreds of islands with these and similarly obvious names, often several in the same lake or bay. Unless there is strong opposition from other local inhabitants, the division will be glad to help you change such a name.

2. There also are a large number of islands which are known by several different names. The division will be glad to help you settle on one of them or, in case no one name is more widely used than another, to establish a new one.

3. A few islands have names which new owners might legitimately find objectionable. Bastards Island, for instance, probably wouldn't appeal to many people. It is vivid and distinctive, which is what the division likes a name to be, but if you bought an island with such a name and insisted on changing it, you probably would get co-operation.

In any of these cases, though, don't forget that you need at least the acquiescence of other inhabitants of the area. If you try to push a change through without first getting them into an agreeable frame of mind about it, you may run into a stone wall of opposition. And the division cannot act contrary to the will of any large group, even if it wants to.

# Public Lands of the United States

Dᴜʀɪɴɢ the last few years the Bureau of Land Management of the United States Department of the Interior has been subjected to recurrent floods of mail from island seekers. Most of the writers had acquired in one way or another the misinformation that the bureau had on hand large numbers of islands which it was anxious to unload on willing citizens. Unfortunately, there is not the slightest truth in this.

The bureau manages some 185,000,000 acres of public land in the continental United States and another 290,000,000 acres in Alaska. It is possible — even probable — that some of this land lies on islands. No one knows for sure. And even if it does include islands, they may not be for sale.

Here is the bureau's official statement on the subject:

Although the original public domain embraced many hundreds of islands, the vast majority passed into State or private ownership during the last great century of land disposal, or are now part of national forests or national parks. Those islands that remain as public domain are often masses of rock, inaccessible, unsurveyed, not classified for disposal or otherwise unavailable to seekers of vacation spots.

The lucky one-in-a-million discoverer of an island who feels sure he has found an island that is part of the public domain must follow a set procedure in claiming it for his own. First, the discoverer must check with the Bureau of Land Management to determine if the island is truly a part of the public domain. If the island is shown on the plats (maps) of the Bureau, and is recorded in the tract books, it will be comparatively easy to determine whether it is public land, and if so, unreserved.

Islands which are public lands are disposed of in the same manner as other public lands — most likely under the Small Tract Act. Before title to islands can be obtained from the Government, however, they must be surveyed by BLM. If the records show doubt as to status of the island — or the island is not recorded at all — the application must contain a statement as to the earliest date the island is known to have existed.

According to provisions of law, islands in inland navigable waters may be considered public land of the United States if they existed above the ordinary high-water mark in the year the State in which they are situated was admitted into the Union and in nonnavigable waters if they were in existence at the date of survey and disposition of the adjacent shore lands. However, if they have formed since the above-mentioned dates, they are not regarded as public lands and the question of ownership is controlled by the laws of the State in which they are situated.

Since an island may be acquired under the Small Tract Act, the "Columbus" who discovers an island or other likely vacation spot on public lands and wishes information on how to acquire such land may get a leaflet on small tracts from any Bureau of Land Management office.

# A P P E N D I X   I I I

# United States Coast and Geodetic Survey Maps

No AGENCY of either the United States or Canadian government is concerned solely or even very greatly with islands. There is, consequently, no one source of general information about all the islands of either country. But the United States Coast and Geodetic Survey (Department of Commerce, Washington 25, D.C.) does concern itself with mapping in detail the coastal islands of this country. (In Canada the Hydrographic Service, Department of Mines and Resources, Ottawa, Ontario, similarly maps both coastal and Great Lakes islands.)

If it is coastal islands that interest you most, the United States Coast and Geodetic Survey maps are the best you can find. There are two chief types. The nautical charts show all off-lying islands and everything else you need to note for navigation purposes, but they are on a comparatively small scale. The planimetric maps are on scales as large as 1:5000 (about one inch of map for every 417 feet of ground covered). The survey will give you indexes of its planimetric maps for any specific area in which you are interested. From the indexes you can get the numbers of the individual maps you want and can then buy them for seventy-five cents each. The survey also publishes eight volumes of *Coast Pilots,* which give text descriptions of the islands encountered in navigating the coasts and a series of charts of the Island (Intracoastal) Waterway, the inside passage along the coast of New Jersey, from Norfolk, Virginia, to Key West and from Key West around the Gulf coast to the Mexican border.

≈≈≈≈≈≈≈≈≈≈≈≈≈≈≈≈≈≈≈≈≈≈≈≈≈≈≈≈≈≈≈≈

# APPENDIX IV

# Electric Power

A GOOD many of the islanders I have met look on island life as a way of getting back to a simple, uncluttered existence. They prefer kerosene lamps for lighting, wood stoves for cooking and an earth cellar for food storage. But the majority, including a good many of those who start out with the intention of rigorously simplifying their lives, find it difficult to get along without at least a few of civilization's gadgets.

Most such gadgets require electric power, and few islands are served by utilities. If you want electric lights, vacuum cleaners, toasters and such, you probably will have to install your own generator. I have found that generators are so far outside most people's experience that the idea of installing one scares them a little. The chief misconception seems to be that a generator is necessarily a huge expense. So here are a few basic facts assembled for me by John Reiner & Company of Long Island City, New York, distributors of Onan Electric Plants.

Prices for gasoline-driven Onan generators start at $219 (F.O.B. Minneapolis). This is for the type you start by hand like an outboard motor. For the type you start by merely pushing a button — which can be located in the house if you wish — add about $70. Add another $70, making a total price of about $360, for automatic controls which start the generator whenever it is needed.

This cheapest generator provides 400 watts of current. That's enough power to run simultaneously all the lights three or four people are likely to need plus a small radio. When the lights and radio are not in use, the power is sufficient to run a vacuum cleaner, sewing machine, fan or other similar small gadget.

If you don't want to be as careful about your use of electricity as this small plant requires and if you want to be able to use a toaster, iron and such, you may have to go as high as 3000 watts. Generators of that much power cost around $600. Electric water heaters and washing machines require generators in the $1200 bracket. An electric stove means an $1800 generator. (Installation costs vary too much from one locality to another for me to estimate them, but they also rise with the amount of power you require.)

My informants don't recommend a generator for power to run refrigerators and home freezers. These require almost constant power, which means either that your generator must run nearly all the time or that you must install an expensive system of storage batteries. Refrigerators — and stoves, too — which run on bottled gas, now available nearly everywhere, are more practical for island use.

APPENDIX V

# Boat Prices

THERE ARE a few islands connected to the mainland by causeways and a number of others in areas where you can rent boats. But I have never met an islander who didn't own a boat whether he needed it or not. Indeed, I know several who have become boat collectors.

To get to and from many lake islands close inshore you can make do with a mere rowboat or even, if you are agile, a canoe. For transportation to others well out to sea you need something sturdy and substantial. To give you an idea of what is available and what it will cost, here are price lists of several widely varying types of ready-made boats of a number of different builders. (These prices are, of course, subject to change, and I can assume no responsibility, financial or otherwise, in connection with any of the boats or firms listed. Prices are F.O.B. the factory, and in most cases crating charges are extra.)

Chris-Craft Corporation
Algonac, Michigan
(Partial list of inboard motorboats — prices are F.O.B. the factory
except last three, on which prices are afloat at factory.)

| Length | Model | H.P. | M.P.H. | Price |
|--------|-------|------|--------|-------|
| 17′ | Sportsman | 60 | 30 | $2,189 |
| 17′ | Special Sportsman | 131 | 40 | 2,690 |
| 18′ | Sportsman | 95 | 32 | 3,047 |
| 18′ | Riviera Runabout | 131 | 38 | 3,300 |
| 19′ | Holiday | 95 | 32 | 3,566 |
| 19′ | Racing Runabout | 158 | 44 | 3,450 |
| 20′ | Riviera Runabout | 130 | 36 | 3,787 |
| 22′ | Sportsman | 95 | 30 | 3,722 |
| 23′ | Holiday | 130 | 33 | 5,474 |
| 24′ | Express | 95 | 26 | 4,503 |
| 25′ | Enclosed Cruiser | 95 | 24 | 5,795 |
| 27′ | Super Enclosed | 130 | 24 | 8,085 |
| 31′ | Express | 2–95* | 25 | 11,404 |
| 32′ | Super Enclosed | 2–95* | 24 | 12,199 |
| 34′ | Enclosed Cruiser | 2–95* | 22 | 13,977 |
| 35′ | Commander | 2–105* | 24 | 16,776 |
| 39′ | DS Salon Cruiser | 2–130* | 24 | 20,884 |
| 42′ | Commander | 2–145* | 23 | 24,592 |
| 47′ | Buccaneer (DCFB) | 2–145* | 22 | 29,833 |
| 50′ | Catalina (DCFB) | 2–160* | 22 | 34,100 |
| 54′ | Motor Yacht | 2–160* | 19 | 54,560 |
| 62′ | Motor Yacht | 2–160* | 14 | 102,610 |
| 62′ | Motor Yacht | 3–200* | 20 | 121,750 |

(G.M. Diesel)

* Reduction drive.

### Boat Kit Division
### Chris-Craft Corporation
### Algonac, Michigan

(Partial list of boat kits, which include precision-cut wood parts, fastenings, seam compound, decals, screw driver and assembly instructions — you do the work.)

| Type | Price |
|---|---|
| 8′ Pram, Kit | $45 |
| Sailing Kit, for 8′ Pram (less sail) | 40 |
| Sail for 8′ Pram | 28 |
| 10′ Utility Racing Pram, Kit | 91 |
| 12′ Runabout, Kit | 112 |
| 14′ Sportsman, Kit | 139 |
| 17′ Speed Boat, Kit | 449 |
| 18′ Outboard Express Cruiser, Kit | 595 |
| 21′ Boat, Kit | 594 |
| 26′ Boat, Kit | 1,274 |
| 31′ Boat, Kit | 1,675 |

### Duratech Manufacturing Corporation
### 198 Main Street
### Tarrytown, New York

(Partial list of aluminum boats.)

| Type | Weight (pounds) | Price |
|---|---|---|
| 9′ Sport Boat | 53 | $157 |
| 9′ Dinghy | 59 | 183 |
| 11′7″ Fishing Pram | 69 | 179 |
| 9′ Sailing Pram | 57 | 329 |

### Evinrude Motors
### Milwaukee 16, Wisconsin

(Outboard motors equipped with Simplex Starters.)

| Model | H.P. | Price |
|---|---|---|
| Lightwin | 3 | $147.25 |
| Fleetwin | 7.5 | 210.00 |
| Super Fastwin | 15 | 325.00 |
| Big Twin | 25 | 396.00 |

Folbot Corporation
42–09 Hunter Street
Long Island City, New York

(Partial list of folding boats with collapsible frame and fabric covering.)

| Model | Weight (*pounds*) | Price |
|---|---|---|
| 16'6" Kayak Single-seater | 54 | $119 |
| 16' Thrifty Two-seater | 59 | 134 |
| 17'6" Super Two-seater | 74 | 179 |
| 15' Runabout Square Stern | 92 | 199 |

Owens Yacht Company
Baltimore 22, Maryland

(Partial list. The cheaper boats consist of little more than hull and cabin. You choose which accessories you want to buy from lists too long to include here.)

| Model | Price |
|---|---|
| 20'3" Outboard Cruiser | $990 |
| 20'3" Inboard Cruiser (without engine) | 1,090 |
| 20'3" Inboard Cruiser (with engine, galley, toilet and other cabin furnishings) | 2,590 |
| 24'4" Inboard Cruiser (with engine and other equipment fairly complete) | 3,390 |
| 30'6" Inboard "Express" (with engine and other equipment fairly complete) | 8,680 |

C. F. Woodcraft Boat Company
410 Lafayette Street
New York 3, New York

(Partial list of wooden boats.)

| Model | Price |
|---|---|
| 12' to 16' Outboard and Rowing Dories | $240 to 340 |
| 12' to 16' Decked Outboard and Rowing Dories | 265 to 370 |

| Model | Price |
|---|---|
| 8' to 16' Master Skiffs (all cedar) | 135 to 215 |
| 8' to 16' Weldwood Skiffs | 105 to 180 |
| 8' to 10' Aero Weight Pram | 125 to 145 |
| 9' The Swan Sailing Dinghy | 350 |

# Boat Builders

$A$PPENDIX V includes only a cross section of widely varying types of boats and their prices — a complete catalogue would be too lengthy. To supplement it, here are the names and addresses of other boat builders scattered around the United States and Canada. This list was compiled by, and is presented with the permission of, Evinrude Motors of Milwaukee, Wisconsin. (Neither Evinrude nor I can assume any responsibility, financial or otherwise, in connection with any of the firms listed.)

The list includes the makers of a wide variety of craft ranging from canoes and rowboats on up in size and price. Some specialize in one or two types, others make many different kinds.

## UNITED STATES

*Arkansas*
Bowman, Inc.
1823 Woodrow St.
Little Rock

*California*
Carver Craft
1750 Newport Blvd.
Costa Mesa

Kelson Engineering Co.
11274 E. Rush St.
El Monte

Kettenberg Boat Works
P.O. Box 65
Pt. Loma Station
San Diego

Rockholt Boat Works
523 J St.
Marysville

*Connecticut*
Alcort, Inc.
1172 North Main St.
Waterbury

Roberts Industries, Inc.
980 N. Main St.
Branford

*Florida*
Forest E. Johnson
325 N.W.S. River Drive
Miami

Kauffman Boat Works
Osprey
  (Winter only.)

*Georgia*
Feather Craft, Inc.
450 Bishop St.
Atlanta

*Illinois*
Ozarka, Inc.
Washington & Borden Sts.
Woodstock

Switzer-Craft
McHenry

*Indiana*
Aero Mfg. Co.
Syracuse

Goshen Churn & Ladder, Inc.
Marine Division
Goshen

Star Craft Metal Boat Co.
101 Star Ave.
Goshen

*Iowa*
Hafer Boat Co.
Spirit Lake

*Louisiana*
Holmes A. Thurmond
100 Block Thatcher
Shreveport

*Maine*
Dunn & Elliot Co.
39 Wadsworth St.
Thomaston

W. D. Heald
Camden

Old Town Canoe Co.
21 Birch St.
Old Town

White Canoe Co., Inc.
156 S. Water St.
Old Town

*Maryland*
Jenkins Marine Motor Sales
327 N. Calvert
Baltimore

George E. Meese
Naval Architects & Marine
   Engineers
1179 Acton Road
Annapolis

Noland Brothers
538 N. Patterson Park Ave.
Baltimore

*Massachusetts*
Cape Cod Shipbuilding Co.
Wareham

Marcus Lowell & Son
High Road
Newbury

Sport Haven Boat Co.
45 Franklin St.
Watertown

A. R. True, Inc.
10 Morrill St.
Amesbury

*Michigan*
Aero-Craft Boats
St. Charles

Bay City Boat, Inc.
304 State St.
Bay City

Century Boat Co.
Sixth Ave.
Manistee

Clyde Boat Co.
8600 Livernois
Detroit 4

Freeland Sons Co.
Box 30
Sturgis

Kauffman Boat Works
Alpena

Squires Mfg. Co.
Milan

*Minnesota*
Alexandria Boat Works
Alexandria

Aluma Craft
2633 27th Ave. South
Minneapolis

Miller-Haxton Mfg. Co.
1408 McKinley St.
St. Paul

*Mississippi*
Marble Boat Mfg. Co.
Lucedale

*Missouri*
General Marine Co.
6th & Oak Sts.
St. Joseph

*Montana*
Ole Lee, Jr.
Somers

Stan-Craft Boat Co.
Polson

*New Jersey*
Fred Jacoby Boat Works
1708 40th St.
North Bergen

Seaman Sea-Skiffs
491 Atlantic Ave.
Long Branch

Westlawn Associates
Montville

Winner Mfg. Co.
Trenton 3

Zobel's Sea Skiff &
Yacht Works
700 Ocean Ave.
Sea Bright

*New York*
W. A. Burnette
1 W. Main St.
Owego, Tioga County

Custom Craft Industries
Division of Marine Mart
Buffalo 7

Dundee Boats
Dundee

C. C. Galbraith & Son, Inc.
99 Park Place
New York

Metal Boat Division
Grumman Aircraft Engineer-
ing Corp.
Bethpage, L. I.

Klepper Company
1472 Broadway
New York 18

Robert B. McKean
180 E. Prospect Ave.
Mamaroneck

Morehouse Boats
Seneca Falls

New York Rubber Corp.
Beacon

Penn Yan Boats, Inc.
Penn Yan

Skaneateles Boat Co., Inc.
Skaneateles

Thompson Bros. Boat
Mfg. Co.
127 Elm St.
Cortland

*North Carolina*
Barbour Boats Inc.
Ft. Metcalf St.
New Bern

*Ohio*
Douglass & McLeod Inc.
P.O. Box 311
Painesville

Ray Green & Co.
Byrne Rd. at South St.
Toledo 9

Inland Seas Boat Co.
3457 West 140th St.
Cleveland 11

Lyman Boat Works
Sandusky

*Oregon*
C. R. Dillabaugh Co.
7928 N. E. Mallory Ave.
Portland

Glen's Boat Shop
333 Oak St.
Grants Pass

*Pennsylvania*
Fleetcraft Corp.
Rockledge
Philadelphia 11

Trojan Boat Co.
Lancaster

*Rhode Island*
The Anchorage, Inc.
57 Miller St.
Warren

Harvey & Kelley
67 High St.
Wakefield

*South Carolina*
Halsey Boat Co.
Bay Front Section
Charleston

Luther H. Smith
Murrells Inlet

*Texas*
Helton Boat Works
6402 Harrisburg Blvd.
Houston

Lone Star Boat Mfg. Co.
1930 Main St.
Grand Prairie

*Vermont*
Edgar Chiott & Son
87 King St.
Burlington

*Washington*
Washington Boat Center
705 East Northlake
Seattle 5

*Wisconsin*
Badger Boat Builders
Couderay

Dunphy Boat Corp.
Broad at Parkway
Oshkosh

Nehls Boat Co.
Portage

Schneider Boat Co.
1913 W. Vliet St.
Milwaukee

Shell Lake Boat Co.
Shell Lake

Thompson Boat Mart
Minocqua

Thompson Bros. Boat Mfg. Co.
Peshtigo

Tomahawk Boat & Mfg. Corp.
Tomahawk

C. S. Van Gordon & Son
218 10th Ave.
Eau Claire

## CANADA

*New Brunswick*
Chestnut Canoe Co. Ltd.
Fredericton

*Nova Scotia*
Plycraft Division
Industrial Shipping Co.
Mahone Bay

*Ontario*
Gordon Boat Works
Bobcaygeon

Lakefield Boats Ltd.
Lakefield

The Peterborough Canoe Co.,
Ltd.
290 Water St.
Peterborough

The Port Carling Boat Works
Ltd.
Port Carling

J. H. Ross Boat Co.
Orillia

*Quebec*
Bastien Bros.
Village Huron

Henry Ross, Ltd.
32 Racine St.
Loretteville

## BOAT PLANS

These firms supply build-it-yourself plans for a wide variety of boats:

Cleveland Boat Blue Print Co.
3107 Detroit Ave.
Cleveland 13, Ohio

Mechanix Illustrated Plans
Service
Fawcett Bldg.
Greenwich, Connecticut

Popular Mechanics Press
200 E. Ontario St.
Chicago 11, Illinois

The Rudder Publishing Co.
9 Murray St.
New York 7, New York

Westlawn Associates, Naval
Architects
Montville, New Jersey

## BOAT ACCESSORIES

This firm carries a complete line of all types of boat equipment:
Oluf Mikkelsen Company
393 Fourth Ave.
New York 16, New York

# Index

# Index

# Index